Making Life Better

The Correct Craft Story

BILL YEARGIN

IGNITE
P R E S S
Fresno, CA

Published in the United States by
Ignite Press
5070 N 6th St. #189
Fresno, CA 93710
www.IgnitePress.us
ignitepress.us

ISBN: 978-1-953655-26-4 (Amazon Print)
ISBN: 978-1-953655-27-1 (IngramSpark) PAPERBACK
ISBN: 978-1-953655-28-8 (IngramSpark) HARDCOVER
ISBN: 978-1-953655-29-5 (E-book)

For bulk purchases, contact:

Correct Craft
learners@correctcraft.com
14700 Aerospace Pkwy
Orlando, FL 32832
407-855-4141

Library of Congress Control Number: 2020923747

OTHER BOOKS BY BILL YEARGIN

Yeargin on Management

What Would Dad Say? Now That He's In Heaven

COMING LATER IN 2021

Education of a Traveler

Education of a CEO

This book is dedicated to all of those who have gone before our current Correct Craft team, constructing the foundation on which we build today. This, of course, includes the Meloon family, but it also includes the thousands of employees who have worked hard at Correct Craft for nearly a century. We stand on your shoulders, and without your effort, we would not be where we are today. Much appreciation.

ACKNOWLEDGMENTS

I also want to thank Ruth Shively and Erica Marrero, both of whom have worked hard on this book and made it far better than it would have been without them—thank you.

TABLE OF CONTENTS

PREFACE

In 1925 when my grandfather founded Correct Craft, I doubt he imagined it would one day be the global organization it is today. Several boat brands, an engine and transmission company, multiple waterparks, an innovation company, and distribution into seventy countries are a result of the foundation he laid nearly a century ago.

Making Life Better is the story of the beginnings of Correct Craft through today. It shares great challenges and great victories. It tells of my family's history of owning and leading the company for eight decades, until we sold the company to my good friend Daryle. It also shares the story of the spectacular growth and results of the past twelve years.

Our family tried to honor God as stewards of Correct Craft. My father, Ralph Meloon, lived to be over 100 and dedicated his life to glorifying God through all he did at Correct Craft. He was active in Correct Craft well into his nineties and well past the time he had any ownership in the company. One of the things my father was most proud of was the fact that Correct Craft continues to spread his passion of stewardship by hosting weekly Bible studies and yearly service trips. I know that through these actions, his legacy lives on.

When Dad transitioned to heaven two years ago, he passed knowing that the company still honored God. That made Dad happy, and me as well.

Ken Meloon

1

A SOLID FOUNDATION

Walter C. Meloon was a man of character, the kind of person you couldn't help but admire. By all accounts he was humble, resilient, and unwavering in his honesty. He also was resourceful, with a powerful work ethic and steadfast faith. It was this special mix of qualities that led W.C., as he was known to his friends, down the path to become founder of what is today known as Correct Craft—one of the world's largest and most successful boat manufacturers.

A gifted mechanical engineer, W.C. Meloon started his first business as a mechanic in two garages he bought in Ossipee, New Hampshire, the small village where he'd grown up and married Marion Adiena Hamm, a close family friend he met in church. Early in their marriage Walter made a public commitment, was baptized, and began to grow in his faith. The early years of married life found W.C. and Marion frequently moving, trying this and that, anxious to learn what the Lord had in store for them.

W.C. was a hard worker, and a fast one, with strong New England Puritan principles. Just *how* strong became clear after he endured two garage fires in the same year with limited insurance. It took five long years to repay suppliers, the bank, and his customers. Working at the foundry owned by his brother Nat, he was able to save enough money to go back and pay everyone down to the last penny, foreshadowing Correct Craft's response to a much longer economic setback to come years later.

Because he loved to tinker with all kinds of machinery, W.C. spent much of his spare time building a boat powered by a Ford Model T engine driving an old airplane propeller. That hobby set in motion the business that was to fluctuate in the ensuing years, from boom to bankruptcy and back again.

■ ■ ■

In 1925 W.C. moved with Marion and their three sons—Walter O., Ralph, and Harold—to Orlando, Florida. He opened a small boat building business in neighboring Pine Castle and called it the Florida Variety Boat Company. It was there, in a state where more than a fifth of the land is covered by water, that W.C. and his employees started building a variety of craft, ranging from sailboats to powerboats and race boats.

Despite the region's many beautiful lakes, the Florida Variety Boat Company made few ripples in the industry during those early years, but its founder had a knack for promotion and he put that talent to work. During the late 1920s, to supplement the manufacturing side of the business, W.C. introduced a variety of water sports to the public.

Towing his sons behind his powerboats in gliders, aquaplanes, and water skis, W.C. generated valuable publicity for his boats. Many of these exhibitions were held on Lake Ivanhoe, near downtown Orlando. The family even put on water ski shows up the East Coast and all across the Deep South, through Tennessee and the Carolinas. These shows attracted buyers to the Meloons' boats and helped W.C. establish a reputation for innovation.

In 1930, as the Great Depression set in, W.C. expanded his services and added "Construction" to the company name. The enterprise became known as Pine Castle Boat and Construction Company. He kept the firm going with side projects that utilized his engineering talents. These ranged from designing and building a system of canals in Winter Park, building and storm-proofing boat houses, and stabilizing sinking homes. He even got the contract to build a dam at Sanlando Spring, complete with thirty-foot-tall slides, creating the area's first "water park."

Meanwhile, the Depression continued to have its effect on the boating industry. Three bank failures cost the Meloons most of their reserves, but they still had employees to pay on Saturdays. W.C. would often manage to sell a few rowboats, sometimes below cost, and divide up the dollars for salaries. One time he even took his wife's last ten dollars to share with his five workers so they could buy groceries.

Fortunately, W.C.'s knack for generating additional income sources resulted in some rather creative ideas. In 1931 family members and crew raised money giving boat rides. Even a twelve-year-old Ralph, the future marine industry "Hall of Fame" legend, took company boats to nearby lakes to help keep the struggling firm afloat. Encouraged by the idea's success, they started making longer trips, stopping at town squares and using a loudspeaker to announce "boat rides for only ten and twenty-five cents!"

As hoped, all of these promotional activities attracted buyers—and eventually the attention of another promoter, Dick Pope, who was in the early stages of developing one of Florida's original attractions. Pope hired young Ralph Meloon to drive him and potential investors through the chain of lakes near what would one day become Cypress Gardens. Ralph was also at the helm of a Meloon boat when Pope took officials from Washington, D.C. on a trip through the property, and they agreed that the WPA would furnish the labor to start the gardens.

When Pope opened the park in January 1936, he bought all of his ski boats from the Meloons, and for nearly half a century they were the exclusive boat provider for Cypress Gardens. During its seventy-three years of entertaining families, the theme park helped elevate waterskiing to a worldwide sport—all while the Meloon family worked to perfect its now famous line of water ski towboats, the eventual Ski Nautique.

It's notable that W.C.'s greatest promotion, waterskiing, indirectly led to the Meloons playing a part in the birth of both show skiing and tournament skiing. The old saying "Necessity is the mother of invention" was clearly at work here.

By 1936, the company's primary focus was constructing powerboats. After hearing a shoe advertisement on the radio exclaiming "The correct heel for your shoe," W.C. thought, why not "The correct *craft* for you?" and the rest is history. Shortly thereafter, the company name was changed to Correct Craft, and incorporated in 1947.

■ ■ ■

Many stories have been told about W.C.'s kindness and character. His mechanical abilities and devotion to work made him sympathetic toward his workers. He loved people and believed everyone should be treated fairly. *Honesty* and *equal treatment* were his watchwords.

W.C. also refused to acknowledge anyone as his enemy. One day when a man with a real or imagined grievance avoided him on the sidewalk as they passed, W.C. walked briskly around the block to engage his "enemy" in friendly conversation. Competitors and creditors found it impossible to remain angry with him. His calmness and serenity often surprised, and sometimes frustrated, his friends.

It was well known that much of this kindness developed with W.C.'s Christian faith, which grew through his friendship with the Baptist minister O. G. Hall, pastor of the local church. They spent hours talking about church business and spiritual matters.

According to his son Harold, W.C. initially worked on Sundays in order to pay bills.

"He said, 'If you owe someone something, you should keep the doors open on Sunday.'" But after the pastor's counsel, Harold said, "he immediately put up signs reading 'No work on the Lord's Day.'"

Soon W.C. found himself able to pay not only his own bills, but also Pastor Hall's college debt. The policy of honoring the Lord's day has remained in place ever since.

This combination of strong character, unwavering faith, solid work ethic, and skill with machinery, plus the Meloon knack for promotion, formed the foundation of an enterprise that would eventually become one of the world's leading recreational boat builders.

■ ■ ■

Final Thoughts

W.C. Meloon passed away when I was just a kid, and well before I joined the Correct Craft family. However, I remember seeing plenty of Ski Nautiques on the lakes of South Florida and dreaming of someday owning one.

Since becoming Correct Craft's CEO, I have often wondered what W.C. Meloon would think of Correct Craft today. Could he have imagined that the company he started had nearly $600 million in sales last year? What would he think about his shop in Orlando that is now a 200-acre, 270,000-square-foot facility? Would he be surprised that his Orlando company now has fourteen locations nationwide, that we're a global company with distribution into seventy countries?

I suspect he would be happy to know he still has family working at Correct Craft, and that his great-grandson, Greg, is now president of Nautique Boats, Correct Craft's biggest subsidiary.

I am sure there is a lot that would surprise W.C., but I suspect he would be most pleased that, in a time when "mission drift" has become an expectation, Correct Craft has kept its mission of "Building Boats to the Glory of God" for nearly 100 years.

2

BUILDING BOATS TO THE GLORY OF GOD

Now into their twenties, the three Meloon sons—Ralph, Walt, and Harold—began to take on a role in the company. Back in the days when people didn't travel much, the boys and their parents drove up and down the eastern seaboard on numerous business trips. This greatly increased their knowledge, and even their teachers agreed it was a good experience. They also had the privilege of working around machines and equipment, putting their natural abilities to good use. Each in his own way, the Meloon sons helped shape the Correct Craft business.

Ralph Meloon once shared in an interview that Harold, his younger brother, started in the business at age fourteen building rowboats. Their father sold them for $16 to $18, and paid Harold $2.50 apiece to build them and .25 cents each to paint them. Since Harold could produce two boats a day, he earned a considerable amount for a teenager. Later, in his early twenties, he designed and installed boat trailers, overhead cranes, and boat dollies, becoming a talented machinist and plant engineer.

"Without Harold," Ralph said, "we would have been in deep trouble. He was the machinist. You don't develop new machines without a machinist."

His older brother Walt was gifted at designing and selling boats—both of which would help propel the company to new heights.

The only brother to graduate high school, Ralph was good with figures, and helped run the business. When World War II started in 1939, he continued to put his business acumen to work for the company, flying all over the country bidding on government contracts.

"Unless you were building boats for the government, you didn't have priority," Ralph explained. And without priority you didn't have access to materials to build them. Because no one could buy gasoline unless they were using it for the government, people weren't interested in buying boats. So we almost died waiting for contracts."

As World War II progressed, in 1942 Correct Craft added a second plant in Titusville, Florida, where they manufactured boats for the war effort. It was there, in 1943, that W.C. conducted his first workplace chapel service as a way to share his faith with family and business contacts, a practice that continues to this day in the form of

Bible study classes for interested employees at Correct Craft plants nationwide.

■ ■ ■

The United States was still at war in December 1944, and families with servicemen overseas faced the Christmas season with fear and uncertainty. But Adolph Hitler overplayed his hand in the Battle of the Bulge. In a massive counterattack against Allied forces staged just before Christmas, his army inflicted major damage, but also suffered heavy losses it couldn't afford. Though many Americans were unaware, the Third Reich had begun to crumble.

General Dwight D. Eisenhower and his forces rapidly advanced, pushing steadily through France, Belgium, and across the border into Germany toward Berlin. Victory seemed near, yet one major setback still stood before them—the Rhine River. Since the time of Napoleon, this swift, muddy river held Germany's enemies at bay. How would the Allies cross the Rhine?

The very success of the Allied drive created another potential problem. Because Eisenhower was weeks ahead of schedule, his armies were approaching the banks of the Rhine without enough boats to make a safe crossing for troops or equipment. The general pondered his strategy. He knew he would face a crucial loss of time and men unless he could cross the river quickly, so he set March 10 as the best date for the operation.

Cabling an SOS to Washington, Eisenhower asked for delivery of 700 storm boats by early March. The compact, 17-foot vessels, with their spoon-shaped bows, were tailor-made for such maneuvers. The highly expendable boats could cross the river and skid up onto beaches at full throttle. It was now early February, and strategic Allied gains could be lost unless they pressed their advantage.

In Florida, Correct Craft was one of several suppliers building boats for the military. In fact, the company had already signed a contract to supply twenty assault boats a month when government officials placed an emergency call from Washington on February 9.

But Correct Craft had shut down that day in honor of a friend's funeral held in a nearby church. W.C. was at the service with his three sons, and when they returned to the plant, the watchman handed him a message: Army engineers had been trying to reach him all afternoon, calling from a district office in Jacksonville, a division office in Atlanta, and the chief's office in Washington, D.C. When W.C. returned the call, the chief engineer explained Eisenhower's situation.

"Look," he said, "here's some classified information so you can understand how important this is. General Eisenhower has set March 10 as the day to cross the Rhine River. We must get as many boats there as possible or our troops will run out of food and all supplies.

"If possible, we need 700 boats. How many storm boats can you build by February 28 with a triple-A preference rating and all the cooperation possible from U.S. engineers?"

W.C. promised to reply after he held a family conference, but what he really wanted was time to pray.

■ ■ ■

The next morning, W.C. called the army man back.

"If God is in it," he said, "we believe it's possible to build 300 boats."

"We didn't know how to build 300 when we said that," Walt later admitted, "but God showed us how."

The firm's normal February schedule called for building forty-eight boats. Retooling and gearing up for *six times* that amount was an impossible task, friends assured them. They would need more workers. Countless male laborers were serving in the military and unavailable, yet the Meloons had confidence in God's ability to do the impossible as they did their part.

The next day, the plant geared up for increased production. The Meloon family and their employees worked until midnight building jigs, open frames for holding work and guiding machine tools to the work. They made preliminary plans to start production. After stopping to rest on Sunday, they resumed work at 1 a.m. Monday. That day, they increased their crew from 60 employees to 320. The company quickly hired scores of women to replace the male boatbuilders who were overseas.

Like the other private contractors making storm boats, Correct Craft faced multiple problems: scarcity of materials, uncertain transportation, new and inexperienced help, and shortage of time. The Army Corps of Engineers sent help as promised, including a plant engineer and a staff of inspectors. Still, only fifteen days remained to complete 300 boats.

The Corps of Engineers helped all the boatbuilders meet the rush deadline. A materials expediter came to Orlando to help locate supplies and specialty tools for the task. The key component was plywood, not in large supply during wartime. The Corps helped the boatbuilders secure sheets of it from Pacific Northwest lumber mills and then had the wood flown cross-country to eastern boat shops. It was winter, though, and in some cases truck drivers with vital supplies had to crawl over mountainous roads through fierce storms. But all the trucks were able to deliver without a single accident. It was an answer to a prayer.

■ ■ ■

Government expediters offered many good suggestions, but one requirement was unacceptable to Correct Craft management. An army colonel asked the company to keep its doors open seven days a week in light of the emergency situation. The Meloons responded with a polite but firm *no*.

"We intend to do the job to the glory of God," W.C. said. "It's not His plan to work seven days a week."

The colonel argued that the company needed the three extra days to accomplish the task, but the Meloons stood their ground, quoting two scriptures: "Remember the sabbath day, to keep it holy" and "Them that honour me I will honour."

The Meloons did not give in, even though they knew a possible legal battle with the government could wipe them out. They pressed the discussion.

"We're working our people sometimes eighteen hours a day on one shift," W.C. told the official. "They can't take it anymore. In fact, God built this world in six days and rested on the seventh. That's what we're going to do, and we're going to trust him for the results."

The company's response surprised the Corps of Engineers. All the other boat makers operated on Sundays, but Correct Craft made sure its people rested on Sundays so they could go to church and have one day of special worship. As the family told the Corps, it made good business sense too, because rested workers are effective workers. Everyone needs time for both physical and spiritual renewal.

"If we win this war, it will be because God wants us to win," W.C. told them. "It won't be solely because of the effort you make, or we make, or anyone else makes. If God wants us to win this war, we'll win it. But if He doesn't, we'll lose it!"

W.C. went as far as offering back the contract if they insisted on working Sundays, telling them that the job was "impossible for man to do alone."

The Corps listened and finally agreed. It dropped the requirement and waited to see if the company would finish the job on time.

Similar conflicts arose at Correct Craft's Titusville, Florida plant. There the Meloons built boats for the navy, including plane rearming boats, navy whaleboats, and plane personnel boats. Government policy restricted awarding contracts to builders that serviced more than one branch of the military at a time. Providentially, the Meloons believe, contracts came from the army and navy on the same day and remained in effect with government approval.

A navy inspector in Titusville told the firm it could not take time out for weekly chapel services, but again the boatbuilders stood their ground.

"If we can't serve the Lord and the U.S. Navy at the same time, we just won't serve the navy."

The navy commander in Jacksonville finally realized the family's unyielding stand and overruled his subordinate, assuring the Meloons that on this issue, they would have no further problems with the inspector.

■ ■ ■

On Monday, February 12 the company built its first storm boat, and what seemed like an agonizingly slow process began to improve. Workers built three boats on Tuesday and seven on Wednesday. Some of their own employees shook their heads in disbelief when the Meloons called a halt for the plant's midweek chapel service. With three of the fifteen work days gone, only eleven boats had been built.

That night, the entire Meloon family met together and prayed more desperately than ever before, asking God to show them the way to complete the job.

Young Walt awakened the next morning with an idea that would speed production: a new machine and a change on the jig. He made the change and Ralph found a man to build the new machine. He needed the rest of the week to complete the work. Meanwhile, with the change on the jig, production accelerated.

On Thursday, February 15, less than two weeks from their deadline, the workers built thirteen boats. On Friday they built seventeen, and on Saturday twenty-one. Still, with six of the fifteen work days gone, only sixty-two of the 300 boats had been built.

The work crew rested again on Sunday, resuming production early Monday morning, February 19. Refreshed by the day of rest, and with the new machine in action, they forged ahead.

Production accelerated, and two days later an army colonel flew down from Atlanta and found boats stacked all over the plant and spilling into the street. With state and village approval, Orange Avenue had been blocked off for boat storage. Later that year, *National Geographic* published a photo of that memorable scene—a street filled with boats and a sign in the foreground stating the obvious: "Road Closed," and in smaller letters, "Detour."

The plant hummed with activity. By now the 320 men and women workers were building up to forty-two boats a day. A local minister presided at the midweek chapel service and invited the colonel to say a few words to the employees. Standing on top of a cutting bench in the middle of the blocked-off Florida highway, the officer looked down into the faces of the workers.

"Men and women," he said, "you have done a remarkable job, and I want to compliment you. I have just visited three other plants in the north where they are working on this same job, and all of them together are not doing what you are doing."

Encouraged by those remarks and a conviction that God was at work, the Meloons and their co-laborers returned to their task with new zeal.

During the second six-day workweek, the inspired and efficient crew built 240 more boats. Miraculously, no rain fell to slow production. At noon on Saturday, February 24, a jubilant crowd of boatbuilders stood on the sidetrack and saw an express train haul away the 306th boat. Having met their quota four days ahead of schedule, the army engineer in charge of the project praised the endeavor.

"There goes our quota," he said, "four days ahead of schedule. Someone other than man did this job. If it had rained only one day, we couldn't have accomplished it."

■ ■ ■

A day earlier, the plant had received a special request from the chief of the Corps of Engineers. Would Correct Craft build another 100 boats? The other three contractors, he said, fell short of their quotas.

The Meloons said yes. With the accelerated operation now in full swing, in the final days of February their workers built another 100 boats. In total, they delivered 406 storm boats. The final 100 boats were sent to New York in fruit trucks, the best ground transportation available at the time, and then flown to Europe.

Made of inexpensive, flexible birch plywood, the boats would slide right onto shore, where ten soldiers could charge up the beach as the outboard engines kept running. The boats were completely disposable, with only one goal: to storm the beach and discharge their passengers.

As it turned out, when the storm boats the other builders produced arrived at the Rhine, the army couldn't use them.

"The specs were wrong, and the engines wouldn't fit," Walt said. "Ours were the only ones built right."

Walt didn't believe the other companies built their boats incorrectly because they had the wrong specifications.

"They had received the same specifications we had," he said. "For some reason, they did not follow the specs; we did, the engines fit on them, and the boats crossed the river successfully."

He speculated that replacement workers at the other companies were either not well trained or not well rested, as they had been given no Sundays off.

The only special preparation the Correct Craft replacement workers had received before they began building the assault boats was to view one already made. Management had bought one from another boatbuilder assigned to the project. They hoisted the craft above a blueprint. It was a valuable model, according to Walt: "Our workers could see it over the blueprint and visualize how to loft (curve) the boat and compare it to their patterns."

Plant workers prayed with extra fervor for the success of the Rhine crossing. The crossing went smoothly. The assault boats, all manufactured by Correct Craft, gave the soldiers several crossing points along the river. The advantage to that approach was that if Hitler's troops were watching the river, the Americans were safer being spread out rather than following one another across a bridge. More than 4,000 sailors crossed in the boats that day.

The Allies got a "bonus" crossing as well. Somehow the Nazis failed to blow up a railroad bridge at Remagen on the Rhine before the Allies arrived. Hitler was furious. Two days later, he executed the three men whom he held responsible for what may have been the greatest blunder of the war.

As the Remagen bridge stayed up, the Americans benefited from continued access to the bridge after the boat crossing, and vital supplies flowed freely. But the boat crossing had been crucial, creating a beachhead that would allow the Allies to move ever closer to Berlin. By May 8, 1945, the war in Europe was officially over.

■ ■ ■

Later that month, the United States military remembered the number and quality of the assault boats produced by Correct Craft and called it a miracle. On May 23, 1945, in a special ceremony at the Orlando plant, the U.S. government awarded the company the Army-Navy Excellence in Production ("E") Award, and in Washington, D.C., the government listed the boatbuilding achievement on its records as "the miracle production."

For many weeks thereafter, visitors from all parts of the United States came to see the factory where a company could build 400 boats in fifteen working days—without infringing on the Lord's Day.

On March 2, just days after Correct Craft had shipped the final boats, the colonel who'd insisted the company work seven days a week returned to the plant. He now stood in front of the shop, tears glistening on his cheeks as he shook hands with W.C. and his three sons.

"You folks certainly have faith in the Lord," he said. "I want to congratulate you."

The Meloon family attributed all honor to the God who led and strengthened them. Describing the outcome, Walt said: "It's called a miracle in boatbuilding. To us, it was simply an indication that the Lord honors the obedience of His children."

■ ■ ■

The Meloons believed that everything they had, from their health to their skills and business profits, came from God and should be returned to him—and as stewards, they gave generously of their resources.

It's no surprise that W.C. expressed the mission of a company founded on Christian principles the way he did. He believed that Correct Craft's goal was "to build boats for the glory of God," and after almost one hundred years in business, this conviction has never changed. To this day, banners still hang in our plants reminding employees and visitors alike of the company's commitment to faith culture, and its lasting mission statement: "Building Boats to the Glory of God."

■ ■ ■

Final Thoughts

"The Miracle Production" story has become an indelible portrayal of the Meloon family and their values. I cannot imagine the courage it took to tell the United States government, during a world war, that they would not work Sundays. To this day that story helps us keep our values intact.

The depth of the Meloon family's integrity was immeasurable. There are few leaders today with that kind of courage, and unless you are tested it's impossible to know if you have it.

3

STAYING AFLOAT DURING TURBULENT TIMES

The recreational boat business prospered in the mid-1940s through 1957. Correct Craft was now making fifty-foot yachts, fishing boats, and, of course, ski boats. The company continued winning contracts from a military that was well aware of Correct Craft's reputation for reliability after the "miracle boats" that stormed the Rhine.

While the builders designed newer and bigger boats, Walt Meloon continued to hit the highways, selling more of the company's products and signing up new dealers. Like many businesses during this era, Correct Craft rode a golden wave.

The future looked even brighter in 1957 when Correct Craft received a government contract for 3,000 assault boats. Things were going smoothly until a corrupt government employee delivered a veiled request for a payoff through double reimbursement. Sitting across the table from Walt and Ralph as they ironed out the details, the chief inspector suspiciously eyed the papers.

"Did you know," he said, "that you're one of only two companies in the whole Southeast who don't have someone on their payroll who carries an expense account to take care of the inspector's expenses?"

Feeling his way carefully, Walt answered that no, he didn't. He knew the government took care of such expenses. The inspector's sullen look made the Correct Craft officials uneasy, and that's when the fateful slide toward bankruptcy began.

Choosing not to confront the government representative, the family moved forward with production. In retaliation, the agent began rejecting boat deliveries and the company didn't receive payment for craft that, in their judgment, were perfectly sound. At one point, eight out of ten boats were rejected.

Concerned that so many boats were being refused based on tiny blemishes that were actually allowed under terms of the contract, Walt and Ralph decided to try an experiment. They took one of the rejected boats, cleaned off the inspector's chalk marks, and sent it back through the line on a later shift. This time it passed.

The silent war continued. At times the Meloons considered giving the man what he wanted. It wasn't that much compared to what the company stood to lose. After much prayer, Walt concluded that to pay him off would be giving in to this man's devious ways, and not trusting in the Lord.

The Meloons tried many avenues of relief and found nothing but closed doors. Rejected boats piled up in the storage yard. Reading the Bible one night, Walt wondered if the Lord had forgotten them. He expressed his concern in prayer, and an inner voice responded: "Have you forgotten the storm boats and what I did for you then?" Perhaps he had lost sight of the miracle production too soon.

With that clear reminder from the Lord, the family decided it would do whatever it could, short of dishonesty, to satisfy the government. By year's end, they had delivered 2,200 approved boats, but 600 rejects remained in the storage yard.

Then came the final blow. A flatcar had just been loaded with forty previously passed boats. Just as the switch engine backed up to the flatcar, the chief inspector suddenly appeared and turned to Walt Meloon. Pointing to the boats, he told Walt he didn't like their looks, and that they should be unloaded and refinished.

That arbitrary decision, unfair as it was, made it impossible to continue. The contract had already cost the company $1 million more than it had received, and Correct Craft now owed 228 creditors a half a million dollars. The bank had withdrawn all of its commitments as well. In an attempt to collect on expenses owed them under their contract, they filed a complaint with the Army Corps of Engineers, but to no avail.

At a special meeting, their creditors heard the full story. Asking for suggestions, the Meloons promised to pay them as soon as possible. One creditor recommended that the firm seek protection under Chapter 11 of the Bankruptcy Act, which allows management to continue in the interest of creditors. Others agreed to that implicit vote of confidence in the Meloon's integrity, and in August 1958 they took that step.

■ ■ ■

Soon, however, the company found itself between a rock and a hard place. They couldn't continue building boats without payment for those they'd already produced. It appeared that they might have to file for bankruptcy and close the company.

Things worsened at the plant, and in a joint effort to ease the situation, every employee agreed to resign, and Ralph and Walt "rehired" those considered essential to the operation. They also initiated cost-cutting measures, but that went only so far.

Though family assets were about even with liabilities, the trend was heading in the wrong direction, and continuing seemed impossible.

Fortuitously, the help they needed to stay afloat came from three vastly different directions.

To tide them over, a loan came from a business friend in Norway, Torrey Mosvold of the Mosvold Shipping Company in Kristiansand. The Meloons met the Scandinavian magnate through a mutual friend, Gus Gustafson, who had left New York in the mid-fifties to become controller of Correct Craft. During the New York and Chicago boat shows, for many years the Meloons sponsored a breakfast for their boat friends in New York. As Gustafson's guest, Mosvold had attended to hear an evangelist speaker he admired. His loan bought them a little more time.

Then came a letter from Pakistan, replete with misspellings and crossed out words, written on what appeared to be newsprint paper. The writer, retired Pakistani Army Major Moodi Farouki, asked for a quotation on boats like those the Meloons had built in 1951 for the U.S. Army. Evidently the U.S. government had given some of the boats to Pakistan.

Not anxious to add more problems to the growing turmoil, the Meloons filed away the letter unanswered. Why go halfway around the world, they reasoned, to seek a partial solution to their dilemma? They had enough problems close to home.

Several weeks later another letter from Farouki arrived, asking them for the courtesy of a response to his previous correspondence. This time, Correct Craft replied immediately, which began a flurry of communications culminating in a $139,000 contract from the Pakistani government. The Meloons had no money to produce new assault boats, but more than 600 quality wood boats with slight or no blemishes were already available. Correct Craft shipped one to Pakistan's minister of defense as a sample, with the notice that many others were ready to ship. An order came back for 239 of the previously rejected boats. Pakistan signed two contracts, including one for six larger boats.

Several days later the Meloons received a 3 a.m. phone call from Moodi Farouki. He told them the U.S. government had sent a man to Pakistan to tell their minister of defense that the Meloons were not honorable, and not to do business with them. Stunned by the accusation, Walt asked what that meant. Without hesitation, Farouki responded that his government was canceling those two contracts.

Initially, the harried Meloons reacted with understandable shock. Their friends in Norway had sent an additional $40,000 loan, which was already spent. Now the Pakistani contracts were being canceled. Where would the firm turn next? True, God had seen them through difficult situations before, but maybe this was too much for Him. Their hearts knew better, but their heads kept getting in the way.

After the initial shock wore off, the Meloons regained their confidence and composure. They had asked the Lord not to allow them to have the Pakistani contracts unless it was truly His will. A cable the following morning confirmed the cancellation. The controller and treasurer insisted on halting production on the boats immediately, but the Meloons remained firm. The Lord had led; they would not lose faith now.

Unknown to them, the Pakistani government had decided to reinstate the contract for the six larger boats, even as Correct Craft had re-inspected and was ready to test the first boat. But the reinstatement notice failed to arrive in the mail. Still, Walt decided to send ten smaller boats, also tested and approved, with the first large boat, hoping Pakistan would accept the shipment.

Ten days later, a check came for all eleven boats. The Meloons decided to send a few more to see what would happen. Back came the checks, with no protest. Correct Craft kept sending the small boats until all 239 of them had been shipped and paid for by the Pakistan embassy. The Meloons' faith had been rewarded again, and as a result, the company enjoyed a new lease on life—at least for a time.

Their third blessing came from a good friend, Bud Coleman, owner of a local automobile agency, who had loaned money to W.C. Meloon on mortgages for the plant property. For about ten years, the family lacked funds to pay even the interest. Whenever they visited with Coleman or he called on the phone, it was to ask for parts for a boat and to ask about the senior Meloons and other family members. Never once did he ask when they were going to start paying, or if he was going to have to turn the matter over to an attorney.

The Meloons never felt uncomfortable in Bud's presence. Finally, the day came when they could go to him and ask what his books showed they owed. Coleman produced a report showing the condition of the account. He had not compounded the interest for the ten years, but had added only each yearly amount of interest and then totaled it with the principal. The Meloons' amazement turned to gratitude to God.

■ ■ ■

Harried and pressured, the Meloons needed friends more than ever during the days of bankruptcy proceedings. Not only did they need a heavenly friend who "sticketh closer than a brother," but also earthly friends who might provide solace, comfort, and counsel. They found many, but one in particular was outstanding.

A.B. Johnson, founder of Orlando's best-known electrical firm, and a blind man with unusual abilities, had known the boatbuilding family through the Christian Business Men's Committee of Orlando. This was an evangelistically-minded group of laymen who carried their Christian witness over into weekdays as they pursued their business and professional careers.

An occasional golf game—with the sightless Johnson often shooting in the eighties—brought the men closer together. Walt Meloon, in particular, spent some time on the links with the electrical executive, and, inevitably, some of the boatbuilding problems came to light. A.B. had suffered through financial straits in earlier years, and now he wanted to help his friends by sharing his invaluable bankruptcy experience.

When he learned that the Correct Craft firm planned to add a badly needed warehouse valued at some $40,000 on its Pine Castle property, A.B. entered a bid from the Johnson Electric Company to do the wiring. Deliberately bidding low to make sure his plans would work, A.B.'s firm secured the contract.

Now entitled to attend the creditors' meetings, often when none of the Meloons had been invited, A.B. "scouted" the meetings for his friends and looked after their best interests. His wise counsel over a period of many months kept the Meloon family from being forced out of management of the firm.

Walt not only kept his sanity in the midst of an "impossible" situation, but also received words of wisdom on how to proceed in the future. He often recounted his warm association with A.B., an important by-product of his bankruptcy trials. To this day, the Meloons consider A.B. Johnson one of the Lord's prime instruments in bringing them successfully through the bankruptcy battles.

■ ■ ■

With that kind of spiritual assistance, the Meloons found their way considerably eased as they struggled through the bankruptcy proceedings. When the creditors called for a hearing in Tampa to have the Meloon family removed from the company's management, A.B. Johnson insisted on riding in the car from Orlando with them, rather than with other members of the creditors' committee.

Attorney Jim Welch and company controller Ray White also accompanied the Meloons. On the way to court they prayed in the car, acknowledging that they'd made mistakes and asking the Lord for forty-five days to get their problems straightened out.

The Orlando contingent arrived in Tampa only moments before the hearing in the federal courthouse building began. Soon it seemed the time had come for the referee to agree with the creditors' attorney. That would put the Meloons out of management, with the company in the hands of a receiver. At this critical juncture, the attorney for the creditors felt he had an important point to contribute to the hearing.

He stated his complaint that the Meloons had distributed $10,000 among their creditors and told him nothing about it. The judge listened, then noticeably stiffened as his face flushed. He had been the one who signed the checks in question!

He responded, rather gruffly, that it wasn't necessary for the attorney to be told what was done, as the court had given the order to do this. Then he pounded his gavel.

"I'll be prepared to hear more on the Correct Craft matter on March 15 in Orlando," he said.

In the car ride home, one of the men suddenly thought to count the number of days before the next hearing. They had prayed for forty-five days. They now had forty-six!

When the time arrived for the hearing in Orlando, the Meloons still hadn't found a solution to the firm's financial problems, so the opening move by the creditors' attorney caught them completely by surprise.

"Judge, I don't know why, but since the hearing in Tampa my clients have asked that I withdraw the complaints."

In three minutes the hearing was over. Another important skirmish had been won.

Regardless, negotiations dragged on for another six years, during which time the judge retired. The court appointed a replacement who promptly notified Correct Craft and the creditors that he was going to liquidate the company in ten days! By this time the small creditors had been paid off—101 of them. They all received 100 percent of what Correct Craft owed.

A letter to the remaining 127 creditors asked a direct question: "Would you accept a settlement of ten percent from the Meloon family within six months, in lieu of the judge putting us out of business?"

All but one creditor agreed. The judge contacted each creditor on his own to confirm the consensus. Satisfied, he released Correct Craft from Chapter 11 of the Bankruptcy Act on the first business day of 1965.

Only a few weeks later the government attorneys for the Corps of Engineers called Correct Craft's attorney, offering a $40,000 settlement if the company would drop its original complaint. The Meloons accepted. Instead of a ten percent settlement with the large creditors, the firm was able to make a five percent payment, followed shortly thereafter by a ten percent payment, and then another five percent payment, totaling twenty percent—twice what the court had directed. It more than satisfied the law, but as time passed, the Meloons couldn't rest without paying back, on their own, the remaining debt to every single creditor.

For the next nineteen years, Ralph led the family in locating and repaying everyone the full amount owed, until finally settling the entire debt in 1984. Finding all the creditors was no small feat. Once, Ralph flew to Michigan after phone calls proved fruitless, and when a creditor had died, Correct Craft chose to spend time searching for the nearest relative to pay, rather than forgetting the debt.

■ ■ ■

Ironically, from Correct Craft's darkest hours also came two key business decisions that helped set the stage for the firm's future success.

During that time a plan was devised to set up regional factory warehouse distribution centers in various regions of the United States. Family members operated most of these autonomous centers, the first of their kind in the boating industry, which proved successful in selling Correct Craft boats to dealers in their areas, and tapped new markets, generating increased income.

"In effect, these five satellite companies acted as flotation barges around a sunken ship, lifting us to the surface," Walt explained. "As a result, Correct Craft became healthy and growing again."

The other key move involved a "newfangled" kind of boat that founder W.C. almost refused to build.

■ ■ ■

Final Thoughts

Correct Craft's bankruptcy story resonates with many people even more than the miracle production story. I believe it's because the story is so relatable and clearly demonstrates both the family and company's integrity.

Who has their debts discharged in bankruptcy and then spends a couple of decades tracking down the creditors to repay them? Not many companies have that kind of story as part of their history and DNA.

4

SETTING THE STANDARD

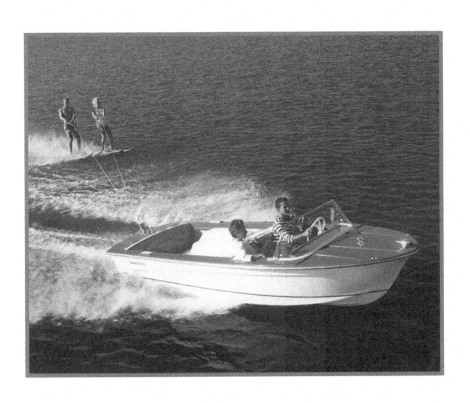

Despite distractions caused by the company's financial struggles, Correct Craft continued building boats. When the introduction of fiberglass brought new possibilities to the marine industry, research and development took off. In 1960 Correct Craft entered the fiberglass era with the Classic, a seventeen-foot towboat. A year later it developed its second fiberglass entry, the Mustang, which had a sixteen-foot length and a narrower hull.

But the recent bankruptcy proceedings had taken their toll, and the company had limited funds for development and marketing of these new craft. Walt and Ralph decided not to tell their retired father about the new fiberglass boats, knowing his aversion to the new material. (This was due partly to the company's first experience with fiberglass technology—namely, the government contract for 3,000 such boats made two years prior.)

Besides, to someone who had been reared on the qualities of wood, fiberglass seemed to contradict the laws of nature. W.C.'s attitude was that since there were no fiberglass trees, there shouldn't be fiberglass boats either.

In spring 1961 Leo Bentz, a Miami ski school operator, offered Correct Craft both the mold to his fiberglass boat and rights to the name for $10,000. Bentz had contracted with a local boatbuilder the previous year to build a new ski boat with a hull designed for a smoother wake. Bentz wasn't a boat designer or a marketer; he was a pre-law student operating three ski schools, yet he sold all twelve of the boats built for him, and the boat was gaining acceptance among top tournament skiers.

With a fiberglass boat of its own, Correct Craft saw little need to add a second one to the lineup. And considering the bankruptcy, "at that point we couldn't have paid $10,000 for anything," Walt explained.

Another factor at play was that Bentz's pitch focused on tournament waterskiing. At that time, the Meloons weren't familiar with tournament skiing, only show skiing, and couldn't relate to the market.

Almost a year later Bentz returned to Pine Castle, but Walt saw him coming and tried to head him off in the street.

"Leo, I'm in no better position than I was months ago," he said.

"I haven't come to sell my boat," Bentz replied, "but to *give* it to you,"

Bentz offered the molds at no charge, as well as use of the name *Ski Nautique* ("water ski" in French). In return, he only required that Correct Craft supply him with one new boat a year for three years, and provide free service to all of the boats he'd already sold. With those terms, Walt relented.

Bentz's bargain was driven by concern for his pregnant wife and the continued demand for his boats. He had let his orders be filled by any boatbuilder willing to quickly assemble two or three at a time, and the quality suffered. Correct Craft represented his major hope of keeping the boat alive, strengthening his schools with new boats and providing free repairs for those already sold.

The Meloons agreed to the deal and started work on bringing the Ski Nautique to market, which turned out to be the company's first step toward financial recovery. And so began the vaunted Ski Nautique—the maiden boat in the modern inboard ski boat industry, and a name that would become one of the world's most recognized boat brands.

■ ■ ■

It was Walt's job to oversee production of the new ski boats. Test runs revealed that the boat handled well, making it easy to drive, even for novice boaters. For those days, it was both comfortable and nice-looking. Skiers holding the tow rope liked the smooth ride, and the broad, flat wake behind the boat was actually superior to that of Correct Craft's own Classic and Mustang.

After they built fifty Ski Nautiques, Bentz's mold had practically disintegrated. Since he already discarded the plug, he had to create an entirely new mold. With room for improvement, the Meloons took the opportunity to modify the design, specifically the deck. Walt eliminated the interior beam that ran across the boat's width. Although it had its purpose, serving as a seat back, a place to secure the ski rope, and a cross beam that helped hold the boat together, it kept the driver and passengers from easily getting from the front to the back of the boat, so it had to go. Walt also added a pylon near midship to attach the tow rope, as well as better throttle controls, and rear-facing seats so passengers could watch the skier.

■ ■ ■

The Meloon sons had built the first fiberglass boats while their father was at the company's New Hampshire warehouse, certain that if he'd been back at the Florida headquarters W.C. would have fought the venture. How did they convince him otherwise?

Knowing that W.C. would never have allowed the project if he was there, Walt and Ralph sent him a finished boat with no explanation. As the story goes, the truck driver pulled up to the warehouse and said, "Mr. Meloon, wait until you see the new fiberglass boat they've built." Later, the brothers shared that they would have loved to have been there and seen the look on his face.

■ ■ ■

Now that Correct Craft had created what one reporter later described as "the most widely used, easily recognized and arguably the best water ski towboat in the history of the sport," it was time to start promoting the Ski Nautique—and that meant getting it into tournaments.

When Bentz initially described the Ski Nautique's strengths to the Meloons, he accentuated the fact that tournament skiers had embraced the boat. The pros—those skiers at the top of the sport who traveled from one competition to the next—approved of the Nautique's performance.

Deciding that interest among the pros was worth pursuing, Walt contacted Bill Clifford, executive director of the American Water Ski Association (AWSA), for advice on promoting the new boat. His answer: "The skiers have to ask for it." So, Walt requested a list of the top competitive skiers and offered each of them a new Ski Nautique at half price if they'd use it at tournaments. All but one took him up on the deal, and tournament waterskiing was forever transformed.

At the time, his fifty percent promotional sale discount was controversial. "People within my own organization thought I was nuts, because we were right on the edge of bankruptcy," Walt said. "But I guess there are just some things it's easier to apologize for than to get permission."

This strategy of putting its boats into the hands of pro skiers succeeded far beyond their expectations. The Ski Nautique began to show up at all the water-ski tournaments—from San Diego to Maine—and the initial offer of half-price boats helped competitive skiers at a time when money purses were light. "I think that had a lot to do with waterskiing's fast growth," Walt observed.

Bill Clifford, who'd been AWSA's executive director for twenty-seven years, said in an interview that he believed part of the company's success with its new fiberglass boat was due to timing. "It's important to note that the sport was coming of age, and the Meloons were definitely in the right place at the right time," he said. But he also noted the Meloons' willingness to do something new. "Just as importantly, they *listened*. I think that's the success story."

As the first manufacturer to develop a relationship with tournament waterskiing, Correct Craft also pioneered the concept of team sponsorship. Under Ralph's watch, they established the first water ski team—champion skiers who received discounted boats and often free accessories in exchange for promotional considerations. That, in turn, gave fans an idea of what water sports and the towboat market were all about. Today, almost all the companies in the industry have a version of this program.

■ ■ ■

Throughout the sixties and seventies, under Walt's leadership, research and development took off. Correct Craft built a new plant down the street from HQ, and staff went full throttle with testing and research on nearby lakes.

Walt's R&D program got the creative juices of all the design people flowing. They also kept Team Nautique members involved, using them to test the results of any changes made. The skiers provided valuable feedback on the product's performance, and were part of the company's devotion to improving the boat with design and technology advances.

Those developments began to pay real dividends in several areas, including one that helps skiers the most: wake performance. "The boat already had 'rideability' and lower wakes," Walt said. But they still wanted to improve the product, and, despite financial constraints, they were able to do so.

"When we started to get some money in, we began to experiment," he explained. "An example is the rudders. We learned a long time ago they have a lot more to do with a boat's performance than people think. Just a couple minutes of grinding the rudder would make the boat steer perfectly. In the late-sixties, we also widened the boat and curled the bottom down and out to keep the spray from passing into the boat. Then we dropped a deeper V in the hull."

Continued innovation throughout the 1970s and early '80s produced an array of runabouts, cuddy-cabin, and center console models, including the Southwind, Martinique, Cuddy Nautique, Fish Nautique, and Bass Nautique. During the 1980s, enthusiasm for towed water sports surged and the company's Ski Nautique and Barefoot Nautique pulled many tournaments around the world. The Ski Nautique 2001 made an exceptional debut in its first year of tournament use, becoming the exclusive towboat at the 24th Annual Masters Tournament at Calloway Gardens, Georgia, and at the World Cup in London.

■ ■ ■

As research and development continued, the company released better versions of the Ski Nautique, and Ralph "the promoter" took to the road on a scale larger than any of the Meloons could have imagined.

During the 1970s and 1980s, Ralph visited eighty-five different nations, promoting waterskiing, building the Correct Craft brand, and sharing his faith. He was instrumental in selling boats to water ski federations in numerous countries, including the USSR and China when access was almost virtually impossible. A deeply religious man, Ralph used the boats to smuggle Bibles into countries that would not allow them.

These promotional efforts laid the groundwork for worldwide distribution of Correct Craft boats.

■ ■ ■

Final Thoughts

Unfortunately, as with W.C., I never had the opportunity to meet W.O. or Harold Meloon. However, I did spend a lot of time with Ralph, and what a man! Before he passed away in 2018 at age 100, he would regularly pop into my office and say something to the effect of "Betty and I love you, Bill, and we are praying for you!" And if Ralph said he and Betty were praying for you, you could take it to the bank.

Well into his nineties, Ralph would see me at the office and say he was driving to Tennessee and wanted to know if we needed a boat delivered along his path. He was always willing to do anything he could to help.

Everyone loved Ralph, and over the years, as I travelled across the U.S. and to dozens of countries for Correct Craft, wherever I went someone asked me about him. He had been everywhere for Correct Craft over the decades, and it was always so obvious he cared for, and left an indelible memory on, everyone he encountered.

But Ralph was best known for his deep faith. From smuggling Bibles into the Soviet bloc in boats, to visiting missionaries on the front lines of Lebanon's civil war, to handing his tracts to anyone who would take one, Ralph was deeply committed to sharing his faith.

5

THE RIGHT WAY TO GET THERE

For Correct Craft, the next decade and a half were marked by hard work and industry under the guidance of a third generation of Meloons. The company's insistence on quality materials, craftsmanship, and production, combined with the inner strength provided by strong family ties and commitment to doing things right, proved to be the leading factors in its continued success.

In 1985, when Walt Meloon retired as president of the company his father founded, Walt's son, Walter N., was promoted from vice president/general manager to president.

W.N. had begun working at Correct Craft's sales office thirty years earlier, in 1955. Except for five years spent with the Martin Marietta Company, he'd been a driving force in the firm's growth. W.N. continued to mature in his business skills even as the company grew, and he was named general manager in 1979, handling, by his estimate, eighty-five percent of daily operations. With his promotion in 1985, W.N. became the third generation to hold that title and the fourth family member to hold the position.

In his new leadership role, W.N. remained committed to the company's enduring values of honesty, integrity, and adherence to Christian ethics. Although working "by the Book" still meant observing a day of rest on Sundays, it also meant a lot more in terms of attitudes and actions.

He strongly believed that Correct Craft's goal was "to build boats to the glory of God," as simply stated by his grandfather. In businesses where the owners or top executives weren't Christians, he explained, the goal was "to make money, to be profitable." Making a profit was important at Correct Craft as well, but it wasn't "the most important thing." W.N. believed that work, profit, and honoring God all complemented one another.

In an early history of the company, W.N. emphasized the consistency of Correct Craft's purpose: "[It] has not changed, neither will it change from that of producing quality recreational boats and servicing our customers at a profit as a means of glorifying God and rendering Him excellent...The business principles, ethics, and morals of Correct Craft come through God's strength, and enable us to stand strong, unyielding to mediocrity."

As W.N. and his management team remained committed to the company's founding values, they faced increasing challenges in two areas that still come with the territory in the water ski industry today: advertising and corporate sponsorship.

In a business where some companies promote their products with strong sex appeal, using attractive women in skimpy bikinis, Correct Craft made sure the models in its ads wouldn't make Sunday school teachers blush. The company carefully monitored its marketing content, particularly the photographs used. The same "wholesome" rule applied to the pictorial content of its annual catalogs and product brochures as well.

W.N. summed up the policy this way: "If I can't take my brochure into the church and lay it on the pew and feel comfortable about one of the little old ladies coming in and looking at it, I've got no business printing it."

The company's second challenge came when it had to say "no" to alcohol sponsors. Since the 1960s, Correct Craft has sponsored dozens of water ski tournaments. In fact, it was the official towboat of the world championships and co-towboat (with two others) of the U.S. Open throughout the 1990s. The company has also been the exclusive towboat of the U.S. Masters since 1973.

In a sport where being named "the official towboat" brings the recognition of being a premier ski boat maker, Correct Craft appreciated its selection, and with its Sports Nautique, it won similar honors at most of the world wakeboarding tournaments in the 1990s, including the 1990 inaugural competition in Kauai.

Yet, one time Correct Craft turned down a chance to sponsor a major series of tournaments; in another instance, it surrendered valuable free publicity as a co-sponsor. It took those actions because of its Christian principles—the company didn't want its name and image associated with alcohol or tobacco products.

The policy has been modified only slightly since that incident. Correct Craft decided to draw the line that it would not participate as an official sponsor when an alcohol company was the major sponsor, nor would it allow its signs to appear near those of an alcohol company.

"We ask that we be listed only as the official towboat of the event," W.N. said. "Even if we give a lot of money, we don't want the name 'sponsor' put on us. It ties us too close. We're not comfortable." W.N. went on to explain: "We are to be in the world, not of the world," paraphrasing John 17:16. "Part of my world includes such sponsors, but we don't have to be that close to them."

The company held strongly to its ethical values. Indeed, W.N.'s statement in the early 1990s—"I don't want to change just for the sake of money"—echoed that of his grandfather, W.C., almost sixty years earlier: "If you have made a decision based only on money, you have made a bad decision." The Correct Craft management team remained committed to its founding values.

Then and now, Correct Craft uses one overriding criterion in its business decisions, whether they're about photos used, changing vendors who supply parts for their boats, or dealing with corrupt government inspectors. The decision *must* be consistent with its deeply held Christian principles.

So strong was its reputation for ethical behavior that Correct Craft was highlighted as the major case study introducing "Ethics in the Business System," a chapter in the textbook *Business, Government, and Society*. Each year, business students at more than 130 colleges and universities read about the Meloons' principled stand against a corrupt government inspector. The company's refusal to pay him off and its insistence on paying back 100 percent of what it owed its creditors marked Correct Craft as a standard-bearer for ethical values in the marketplace.

"Correct Craft is a company which is driven by ethical values," wrote the book's co-author, George Steiner, in the eighth edition. "These values, derived from the philosophy and examples of its founder, permeate the company culture to direct employees and influence strategic decisions." Steiner, emeritus professor of management at UCLA, concluded, "[Correct Craft's] story illustrates how ethical values can have a continuous impact on the fortunes of a business." (Note: this textbook is still in use today, though with newer case studies.)

■ ■ ■

Doing things the right way didn't apply just to ethical behavior at the company. It permeated everything they did. For Correct Craft, the "right way" included building a quality product using quality materials. Profit was always secondary to quality.

"When numbers and money become the motivating factors of this company, it's wrong," W.N. once stated. "I don't think it's wrong to want greater revenue and profit. What *could* be wrong is how we get there. You make a decision on the right way to get there."

Production vice president Mike Elrod, a valued employee for close to thirty years, was a firm believer in *quality first.*

"In our society, there are a lot of people and companies that don't care how they achieve profits; they just want the bottom-line profit," he stated. "The Meloons aren't that way. Sure, they like to make money. But they won't cut corners to do it. The quality of the product we build is second to none. What we put into the parts of the boat you don't see is just as good as what you do see. A lot of companies don't do that. I think that contributes to their longevity and their stability."

Elrod explained the company's strong, stable sales in the 1990s this way: "Once we've got the potential customer in the product and he finds out how good it runs, how solid it feels, and the beautiful wake behind it, he gives it a long look." And the company's "being in business for more than seventy years and how we have treated people" gives it a good reputation among customers, he added.

This philosophy paid off for Correct Craft, which at the turn of the century was producing as many as one-third of all inboard ski boats in a given year. Fewer than twenty percent of Correct Craft owners bought their boats for tournament competition. The typical buyer used a Nautique for recreational skiing.

■ ■ ■

Dating back to company founder W.C. Meloon, the firm's primary goal had always been to build better boats. W.N. reinforced this commitment when he wrote in the 1997 catalog, "[W.C.'s] tenet for doing business was very basic—'Offer your customer the best product, the finest materials, and build it to the glory of God.'"

The company succeeded at building quality boats using better materials and designs. And while Correct Craft didn't always pioneer new developments, they often improved on established technology.

"We don't make change for change's sake," W.N. said, describing the company's attitude toward change. For example, he explained, the firm delayed adopting fiberglass stringers for several years, "until we knew more about it, understood it, and could make glass stringers that we could fill with foam and then make the stringers a part of the boat, not set them in a compound or a glue as separate units that you hope stick together. We wanted them to be a permanent part of the boat."

Correct Craft stringers were bonded to the boat exclusively with fiberglass, a more expensive but stronger adhesive than glues or other compounds many companies used. Similarly, another manufacturer introduced AME 5000 resin and several boatbuilders used it on the outer skin. But Correct Craft was one of only a few boatbuilders that made the entire boat out of AME 5000.

Reflecting its commitment to improving existing technology, the company also increased the angle on the reverse chines on its 1997 Ski Nautique. The greater angle reduced the amount of spray behind the boat, which helped skiers on a shorter towline.

Several other refinements to the 1997 model earned that boat's design the term "revolutionary." The package, which the company called Total Surface Control (TSC), included a hull with enhanced spray relief pockets, a streamline bow, a tapered transom, and a new keel relief pocket, in addition to the modified reverse angle chine. All helped to redirect the water flow over the hull, giving a low and smoother wake, which skiers liked, and improved tracking for easier handling, which drivers appreciated.

The final ingredient in the package was a new progressive-pitch, four-blade propeller to increase acceleration—replacing the three-blade as the standard driving force. Correct Craft had challenged its supplier to come up with a four-blade prop that didn't lose speed on the high end.

The California company shipped several variations of a new four-blade design, finally finding the winner in a progressive-pitch propeller. The progressive pitch made the propeller more efficient, increasing thrust. Correct Craft was the second boatbuilder to adopt the four-blade propeller. But it was the first to use the progressive pitch to increase thrust. The new propeller was better accelerating, smoother, quieter, and had the same top speed as the three-blade prop.

In 1997 Correct Craft added another big win to its portfolio. With the focus on "no wake" having shifted to creating mountains of water behind the boat for kneeboarding and wakeboarding, the boat maker introduced its Air Nautique, the first wakeboard-specific boat, which offered the company's patented Flight Control Tower and internal ballast tanks as standard features for big air.

■ ■ ■

SeaWorld was one of Correct Craft's most enthusiastic supporters during the 1990s, contracting with the company to provide boats for water-ski shows at its parks in Orlando, Cleveland, San Antonio, and San Diego.

SeaWorld officials offered heavy praise for the Nautique line, stating that the towboats were the strongest boat they'd ever used in terms of maneuverability, power, and safety. "From my exposure to a wide variety of ski boats," said Jim Timon, former entertainment director of SeaWorld's California park, "the Ski Nautique is by far, hands down, the best there is. You wouldn't believe what these boats go through. The Correct Crafts have never given us a moment of worry."

The towboats proved their worth year after year in SeaWorld's laboratory of quick starts, stops, fast turns, and steady speeds for the ski performers. In an average year, skiers performed two or three shows most days, but they did up to five during the summers to accommodate the vacation crowds. And while the skiers changed, the boats went on show after show after show.

In 1994, for example, Correct Craft boats were driven 304,467 nautical miles during 662,415 shows at the four parks. The drivers and skiers put the boats through their paces, with 420 engine shifts per show and more than ten million engine shifts per year.

The strongest endorsements tended to come from the skiers themselves, who rode behind Nautiques every day. During the 1980s and 1990s, Terri Garner performed for eleven years at the Florida SeaWorld.

She was so impressed with the product that she bought one herself, a 1989 Ski Nautique.

"As an owner," she said, "I'd rather pay more and have something that is good quality, reliable, and the best-driving boat to ski behind."

She was pleased to learn that the boat, which she bought used, had kept its value. After five years of ownership, Terri reported that it hadn't depreciated even a single cent from the purchase price.

"People who want the best quality [typically] buy Correct Craft," Terri explained. "Some people may not know the difference, [but] in the way they drive, in the way they ride, there's no comparison in my mind."

■ ■ ■

Final Thoughts

One thing I really appreciate about Correct Craft's history from the '80s and '90s is the emphasis on quality and innovation. Both values have become embedded in Correct Craft's DNA.

Quality played a big part of building the brand enthusiasm we now enjoy, and our history of building top-quality products serves as a guide for today's Correct Craft team. We know people expect the highest quality from us, and we work hard to live up to and exceed that expectation.

We also love innovation. Correct Craft has won most of the industry's innovation awards, and for the past two years was recognized by Soundings Trade Only as the boating industry's "Most Innovative Company." We are honored and happy to stand on the shoulders of those who came before us and built such a great foundation for our company.

6

TIDES OF CHANGE

Two years into the twenty-first century, Correct Craft began a transformation that would forever change the company. For more than seventy-five years, a Meloon had presided over America's oldest family-owned boat building company. Then, in 2002, W.N. Meloon stepped down and the corporation was led by five different CEOs over five years. For close to a year during that time, Correct Craft was managed by the board's executive committee as they struggled to find the right leader.

This time of transition was perhaps the greatest test of the company's resilience to date; but progress never stopped. Nautique continued to lead the ski/wakeboard segment of the industry in overall customer satisfaction. And despite the financial losses suffered through Hurricanes Charley and Frances in 2004, Correct Craft carried on. Manufacturing up to 2,300 units a year across eight different ski and wakeboard models, the company continued the traditions that made it a success.

With this momentum, Correct Craft began construction in 2005 on Nautique's new 217,000-square-foot manufacturing facility, located on 137 acres in Orlando's International Corporate Park complex. In addition to housing corporate offices, research and development, and manufacturing operations, the project called for the creation of two lakes. One would be used for testing every Nautique prior to its being wrapped and shipped, the other for R&D, as well as hosting water ski and wakeboard tournaments.

In June 2006, the team's 400 employees relocated to their state-of-the-art factory and world headquarters. This innovative complex provided for increased employment and the capacity to produce more boats, allowing for plenty of future growth.

Part of this planned increase would come from changes to the manufacturing process itself. At the old plant, boats were built in a batch fashion, which meant significant idle time in the production process. Boats manufactured in the new facility would move through it in a synchronous flow, combining the work of several departments in each section of the line and speeding up the assembly process.

■ ■ ■

Two months after the big move, Correct Craft's board made the announcement that I had been hired to lead the company as president and CEO starting September 14, 2006. This decision, along with the brand-new facility, marked a new strategic beginning for the company.

When I took over as the fifth CEO in as many years, Correct Craft was going through a difficult transition from family to professional management. The mission was a tall order: stabilization and the creation of a strong foundation for the future. It included realizing Correct Craft's economic potential, while maintaining the heritage of an eighty-three-year-old corporation built on a foundation of faith, ethics, and integrity.

A bit daunting, yes, but these values appealed to me, and I was excited about the opportunity to join the team. The company's culture was consistent with my own, and I looked forward to providing the necessary guidance to ensure its continued success.

■ ■ ■

When I first arrived, there was a lot of confusion related to the company having five CEOs in as many years. There was also some uncertainty among the employees and dealers. Correct Craft was a great company, but during the preceding ten years they'd missed a lot of opportunities to improve. Fortunately, we were able to make the changes that needed to be made, and the positive impact of our actions came quickly.

The development of the company's first-ever strategic plan was at the core of those changes. It was our top priority the day I walked in the door. Correct Craft was obviously effective at building an awesome brand, developing and producing great product, and generating incredible customer loyalty, but we needed a strategic plan to build the company to its true potential and sell the industry's best ski and wakeboard boats.

While crafting and preparing to execute on this long-term plan, we started the transformation with a series of initiatives: the creation of our own lean production system, recruitment of a new wave of executive talent, expansion of our dealer network, and the launch of an employee development program.

Stabilization was the short-term goal. Part of this process involved evaluating the company's more than 400-employee team and ensuring that the right people were in the right positions. I knew we had good people, and my job was to determine whether they were the right people for the right job. Fortunately, we had the opportunity to promote several of the company's long-standing employees, including two fourth-generation members of its founding family.

Great grandson of founder W.C. Meloon, Greg Meloon was charged with overseeing product design and development. A key focus during this period was to make sure we were building what our customers wanted. We took steps to ensure that Correct Craft stayed on top of the trends and embraced new ideas that would lead us into the future. Greg did a great job in this new role.

On the production front, while the new plant had been set up for more modern manufacturing, we still had to perfect the overall process. One of our most significant improvements was the development of the Nautique Production System. This program not only improved the production process and quality control, it also engaged employees, through Villanova University, with a Lean Six Sigma course, a more open communication practice, as well as pay raises for *Boat Building 101* graduates, our in-house training program open to all employees.

This culture of continual improvement didn't end there. The company also made a heavy investment in developing our team to solve problems and improve customer satisfaction. Our philosophy was that if team members are happy, respected, and educated in a positive work environment, they work harder and ultimately build better boats.

Just as important, employee comfort, safety, and working conditions were also top priorities. The new facility was built with a large break/entertaining room where employees could enjoy breakfast and lunch. In addition, a sophisticated cross-ventilation system helped make working on the plant floor more comfortable during Florida's long, hot summers.

Our focus on creating the right culture didn't stop there. While organizational values and maintaining a culture of continual improvement are great, I also believed it was important that we did our best to personally live out our values. Soon after arriving at Correct Craft

I started voluntary weekly Bible studies in both English and Spanish, and had the privilege to personally teach the English-speaking groups. The weekly meetings began small but quickly grew.

I also took this opportunity to elevate Correct Craft's community and voluntary faith-based practices to include international service trips and more local community charity work. Our first project was a service trip to Tecate, Mexico with a team of twenty-one employees, to build a house for a family of seven. The project was so well received that the team wasted no time planning a second trip to Mexico, where the following summer we built a home for another family. We also traveled to Nicaragua, Haiti, Guatemala, Ethiopia, Uganda, Kenya, Cambodia, India, and many other other countries to serve those in need.

To this day, the company still organizes and funds international and domestic service trips for interested employees. These trips are a highlight of our year!

■ ■ ■

To help finalize the company's strategic plan, I involved the people who would be responsible for carrying it out. While it's always important to include team members in the planning process, I knew in this case it would be essential. For several weeks in a row I invited groups of employees to my house for daylong planning sessions. We also spent some time team building out on the lake.

The end result, completed in November 2007, was a ninety-seven-page binder listing the ten overall goals for the company and ten for each individual division, with outlines detailing the steps to reach them.

While creating the company's strategic plan was gratifying, our biggest accomplishment during this time was the diligence with which each department set about meeting their goals. Five months into the plan we were already ahead of schedule.

One of our primary objectives was to improve product quality by reducing the number of defects, as measured by an outside quality and reliability rating company. Not only did we improve our results over the previous year, we also demonstrated the best quality in the ski and wakeboard niche, and the second-best quality in the entire boating industry.

I've always told our team, "No matter how good we get, we must get better. We cannot be satisfied with our past accomplishments; we need to build on them." We were clearly on our way to bigger and better things.

■ ■ ■

While our leadership team worked through the process of stabilizing the company, I spent a considerable amount of time managing Correct Craft's transition to new ownership. Many individuals in the Meloon family thought the best decision in the long run would be to sell the company to someone who could invest in it and help Correct Craft reach its potential. They had been selling their shares over a period of years to longtime board member Daryle Doden, owner of Ambassador Enterprises.

The founding family gave up ownership of Correct Craft when they completed the sale to Doden in August 2008. They felt comfortable he would embrace the values that were so important to everyone at the company.

Fortunately, many in the Meloon family remained with Correct Craft after the sale and continued to play key roles. Our chairman emeritus at the time, Ralph Meloon, who at age ninety-two still came to work every day, was an incredible supporter who encouraged the team. Our board chairman was (and still is) Ken Meloon. His experience continued to help keep us on track.

Ironically, the company achieved stabilization with the sale just as we were about to weather a new storm. Little did we know then that the economy was on the brink of what would become the deepest recession since the Great Depression.

■ ■ ■

In September 2008, Correct Craft began to feel the effects of the downturn. The previous year we had built roughly 2,500 boats. By the end of 2008, we were down about ten percent for the year. It was clear that the Great Recession was just around the corner.

Then, during the first quarter of 2009, we experienced a significant slowdown. There was no doubt that, once again, Correct Craft's resilience was about to be tested. When it finally hit, the global economic collapse substantially impacted our industry. Nationwide, new boat construction was off over eighty percent from the previous year. Boat builders everywhere were severely squeezed, and we weren't exempt. At one point our production dropped ninety percent and, while we were not as adversely affected as some, we still had to navigate through a difficult stretch.

Fortunately the changes we'd made before the collapse, combined with a continued focus on improvement, helped us get through those tough times. We worked hard to re-invent our business model, and made some difficult decisions to ensure that the company would survive the recession.

This initiative began with a major restructuring of the company's distribution strategy. We closed our regional warehouses, which were mostly owned by Meloon family members, and began selling directly to dealers to streamline the process. We also changed how we handled dealer meetings. Instead of a several-hundred-thousand-dollar, multi-day event, we moved to an intense one-day training session, which the dealers actually preferred.

Like everyone else, we focused on cutting costs by balancing production to the marketplace. We slowed down manufacturing in order to stretch out the production schedule and expand our backlog, which allowed the company to break even at a drastically lower volume.

We also saw this as an opportunity to invest in our employees and gear up product development efforts, in order to position Correct Craft for the future.

For starters, instead of sending people home, we implemented some unique training and community outreach projects. Early in the year we got creative and offered an employee development program that allowed us to keep people working. Even though we were building boats just one day a week, the rest of the week we held eight-hour classes on various technical and life skills. These ranged from English as a second language and personal finance, to welding.

In addition to training our team members, we dedicated some of these non-production days to community service. One of the beneficiaries was Coalition for the Homeless of Central Florida. In February and March, Correct Craft employees swarmed onto the Coalition's campuses, completing a variety of needed services, such as painting hallways and lobbies, landscaping, and stuffing hundreds of envelopes.

"Even while they were cutting back on expenses, Correct Craft figured out a way to give back," observed Coalition's director, as she expressed her appreciation for their involvement. "The best part was that they did it with all the effort they would normally give a full day's work. They gave it their all."

Sadly, in spite of our best efforts, the boating market continued to deteriorate, and we were forced to let people go. Everyone who left received two weeks' severance, and we delayed the last seventy-five lay-offs as long as possible. It was a difficult time for everyone, especially our human resources director, Shirley Adams—her father was one of the laid off employees. Fortunately for both of them, she convinced him to retire early, and managed to avoid letting him go.

Despite the recession, the company had to maintain product development. In the worst time of the global recession, when most boat manufacturers were cutting back, we took a contrarian approach; Greg Meloon and his team spent more than a year developing several innovative new products.

Our accomplishments paid off when we introduced the Ski Nautique 200, which took the industry by storm. I give credit largely to Ken Meloon and decorated water skier Andy Mapple, who pushed me to approve development of a new ski boat, despite diminished sales industry wide. They had the vision to see what could happen with a revolutionary new towboat, proving once again how important it is to be both product- and future-focused.

■ ■ ■

By late 2009, boat sales began ramping up again, but the towboat sector had taken a huge hit. Industry production had dropped from 13,000 to 4,800 a year. When all was said and done, Correct Craft had gone from a high of more than 400 employees to a low of 125.

Knowing it would be a long time before our industry got back to the unit sale levels of just a few years ago, in May 2010 we re-engineered our business model to be profitable in the "new normal." We also continued developing programs that would make our dealers more effective. Relationships are important to us, and dealer relationships are especially important.

Additionally, we used this time to make necessary changes to position Correct Craft for the future. The results went a long way toward shaping the company into what it is today.

First, we instituted an incentive plan that rewards every single employee when the company does well. This program has significantly reinforced our culture of continuous improvement. Highly energized employees are paid draws on their annual incentive each quarter (and they love getting those checks).

We also brought international distribution in-house. For the next three years I personally traveled to about fifty countries to establish new dealers and beef up export sales in a flagging domestic market.

The company explored new avenues for growth, including opportunities to acquire other marine industry brands. However, we discovered that the timing wasn't yet right. Valuations were either too low and companies didn't want to sell at that time, or asking prices were too high. This would soon change.

■ ■ ■

While taking time to reflect back on this period of Correct Craft's history, and my part in it, I came across an interview I did with one of our industry's newsletters. I thought it would be fun to share my answers to some of the questions here. They nicely sum up my initial years with the company.

What has your biggest challenge been?

The biggest challenge by far has been leading through what may have been the largest collapse ever in the boating industry. Fortunately, our team was up for the challenge and Correct Craft has come out of that time a much better company.

What accomplishment are you most proud of?

If I had to pick just one, I would definitely say my proudest accomplishment is the incredible team we have built. As leader I get to hear the accolades when things go well but, frankly, I play a very small part. The real work is done by our incredible team who loves our company and lives the Nautique life. We have people in all areas of our company who are passionate about our product and pleasing our customers, and that makes my job easy.

What is your most gratifying experience about being CEO, and what do you like the least?

Probably the most gratifying aspect of my leading Correct Craft is helping the company live out our culture of faith. The company has always talked about a faith culture, but I can truly say we are now living it out. Probably the thing I like least is when we have to make people changes. That keeps me up at night, but I know we have to do what is best in the long run for our company and customers.

■ ■ ■

Final Thoughts

I was the fifth CEO in five years, and these five years were some challenging times for the Correct Craft team.

After living my entire life, including college years, in South Florida, I couldn't imagine living anywhere else. Plus, our family was totally embedded in the community. I was chair of our county's hospice, on the board of the community's university, and my wife and kids were involved in all kinds of activities.

We were in love with South Florida, and I thought my next career move was starting a consulting firm. Moving to Orlando and taking the Correct Craft job bordered on the unthinkable. However, I have never in my life felt more called to do anything, and the way the circumstances lined up to make it happen still gives me goosebumps when I think about it. The first three years were excruciatingly difficult, and I sometimes questioned my decision, but I never questioned that Correct Craft was where I was supposed to be.

7

NEW OWNER

The Meloon family did something that very few can. They started with nothing and built a brand and company that is highly respected around the world. They laid the foundation we have used to substantially grow the company. Whenever I'm asked about the success we've had, I always mention that what we're accomplishing is on the shoulders of others, especially the Meloon family. I have tremendous respect for all the Meloon family members, and particularly the leaders, W.C., W.O., W.N., and Ralph.

However, as detailed in the previous chapter, when I arrived in 2006 the waters were troubled. I was the fifth CEO in five years and people were not shy about telling me I wouldn't be there long. The evening before my first day I came into the office and the controller asked if he could see me alone, then proceeded to inform me the financial situation was far worse than I'd been led to believe. My first two days working were spent in a board meeting. It was crystal clear that there was no agreement on where Correct Craft was heading nor how (or if) we would get there.

After the meetings I told one of our board members that the board could either follow or fire me, but I was going to make the necessary decisions in order to survive. During my first few weeks at the office I arrived early and most nights didn't leave until 9 p.m. I was working hard to get an understanding of our situation and taking the first steps we needed to survive. While I was doing that, there were still challenges at the ownership level that seemed impossible to fix. After a few months on the job, I realized the situation was unsustainable and decided to share my concerns with a man I had quickly grown to trust and respect: Ken Meloon.

Ken, grandson of Correct Craft's founder W.C. Meloon, served as our board chair, and he also ran our Midwest distribution center. I knew Ken cared about the company's future, so one evening we sat on the back patio of his Orlando home and I was as transparent as I could be. I reassured Ken that I wasn't threatening to quit, but also told him the current situation was unsustainable. Ken listened carefully and we both realized that Daryle Doden could help Correct Craft.

President and CEO of Ambassador Enterprises, a legacy-minded private equity firm, Daryle Doden founded Ambassador Steel, which was the largest independent steel rebar fabricator and distributor in the U.S., with annual revenues surpassing $500 million. Daryle had also been the largest non-Meloon family shareholder after Ralph Meloon entrusted him with his shares at a time he needed to sell. Ken trusted Daryle, and so did I.

In February 2008, after a few months of discussion, Ken, his wife Diane, and kids Greg and Mindy—who had all been helpful during this tough time—sold their interest in both Correct Craft and their distribution center to Daryle, giving him more than fifty percent of the company's stock. In the months that followed, Daryle acquired numerous other family members' stock, and by August 2008 he owned 100 percent of the company.

Daryle's acquisition of Correct Craft had assured us the stability we needed to grow, but only a month after he acquired all the stock, it was not looking like a very good investment. In September of 2008 the Great Recession arrived and our company lost ninety percent of its business in the months following. While our team was able to navigate the downturn without requiring Daryle to invest more money into the company, knowing he was there and the stability he brought provided a major tailwind during that turbulent time.

Since the darkest days of 2008 and 2009, Daryle has been an exceptional owner. Not only does he embrace the core values that the Meloon family built Correct Craft upon, he has also demonstrated tremendous trust in our team by giving us the autonomy to deliver financial, cultural, and eternal returns way beyond what anyone could have imagined in 2008.

Personally, Daryle has been an invaluable thought partner with me as we've grown Correct Craft. He always stimulates my thinking, and I have learned a tremendous amount from him. Daryle and I have grown to be trusted friends, and I am happy to serve as a trustee on his family trust.

■ ■ ■

Final Thoughts

The Meloon family did what few people can do—they built an incredible brand and company. I believe Ken Meloon may have saved our company through his willingness to listen and act at a very difficult time.

Daryle Doden was the right owner at the right time for Correct Craft. I deeply appreciate his willingness to step up and invest in us.

8
MAKING LIFE BETTER

While the Great Recession was painfully difficult for our company, it also helped us create a foundation that would result in record-breaking results over the next decade. In less than ten years, we've grown from a small, single-brand business to a global organization with eight boat brands, three engine brands, three of the world's largest boat and cable parks, and a subsidiary solely devoted to innovation. We have fourteen locations around the U.S. with manufacturing facilities in six states, and we work with distributors in about seventy countries. Our events now promote watersports, boating, and fishing all around the globe. It has been one of the most exciting periods in the company's history.

With the recession behind us, we were in just the right position to provide our customers with great boats by making what we already had even better, *and* to use the proceeds of those sales to make the world better. We did this by focusing primarily on product and people—because without good product and good people, nothing else matters.

An important part of my job and leadership style is creating the right culture at Correct Craft. We have a high-energy performance culture that also highly values service. In late 2012, we created what I call the "Correct Craft Identity Pyramid." It's based on those timeless principles that define the company and represent the culture we strive for every day. I love the pyramid because it clearly captures both what is important to the company and how we conduct ourselves. We use it often to share this message with new employees and others outside the business.

I can't overstate how critical organizational culture is to Correct Craft, and this pyramid captures our most important values. It starts at the top with "Building Boats to the Glory of God," which was the mission of our founder, W.C. Meloon, and has been the one constant throughout the company's history. This mission is still embraced by our team more than ninety-five years later.

Out of this mission flows our "Why," which is "Making Life Better." This philosophy permeates all we do, and hardly a day goes by that I'm not in a meeting where it's mentioned. We want to make life better for everyone with whom we come in contact, including our customers, employees and their families, dealers, vendors, strategic partners, and people around the world we may only meet once.

Over the years, our "Why" has become a significant part of the company's culture. It forms the basis for providing a positive work environment for employees; for creating great products for our customers by making what we have better; and for using our resources to make the world a better place. This philosophy has earned a strong employee response. People want to be part of something that has a higher mission, and our team fully embraces the concept of "Making Life Better."

Finally, the base of the pyramid represents what is essentially the foundation for everything that lies above. It's our "How." We achieve the goal of "Making Life Better" by focusing on the three pillars of our company: People, Performance, and Philanthropy. I'll be going into more detail about these pillars in the following chapters.

■ ■ ■

BUILDING
BOATS TO THE
GLORY OF GOD

The culture we foster played a major role in Correct Craft's recovery as we came out of the recession and started to move forward. Over the past several years, the company has been "Building Boats to the Glory of God" while following a multi-pronged growth strategy: *continuous improvement of existing product lines, expansion of international markets, acquisition of companies with significant growth opportunity,* and *creating new technologies.*

As the economy turned around, a large part of our attention was redirected toward growing organically through optimization—in other words, continuously innovating to improve everything we do.

In caring for our customers we took on the challenge to improve the Nautique product line, which already had the best-performing boats in the industry. To retain our loyal customers, we worked on enhancing product quality, our industry-leading warranty, and the service levels provided by our dealer network. We also gave customers the option to customize their Nautique, which required changes in the manufacturing process. By introducing exciting product innovations like these, we attracted a broader niche of new boat buyers and expanded our market.

In addition, the company brought on a dedicated quality assurance team and a group of industrial engineers, whose job it is to ensure we always provide top quality. These efforts paid off big time. Nautique consistently won every customer satisfaction award offered in their category, and our Nautique dealers were regularly recognized as the best in the industry, with many landing on the industry's Top 100 list every year.

It was during this period that Nautique kicked off the era of big product launches with the introduction of two new wakeboard boats. In 2012, we won "Manufacturer of the Year" and "Most Innovative Product" after the launch of the Super Air Nautique G23 and G25.

One of our core values is to be a market *driving* company, not market driven, and that mindset makes a huge difference. The G series boats were the best in the industry, and the fact that our competitors were buying them to figure out how to compete with us was a huge compliment. We don't want to copy what someone else is doing, we want to innovate. And by the time someone else catches up, we're on to something else. This is what drives us.

■ ■ ■

We also continued working to expand our international markets in support of the company's growth strategy. To keep up with changing times, we focused on the long view and relationships that would ensure Correct Craft's future success.

After setting up a new strategic international initiative, we began to develop our brand globally. My role was to travel to more than fifty countries, opening, developing, and understanding markets. As part of that process, I established key relationships in each country, meeting with government officials, industry leaders, and others. This led to many interesting experiences, including meeting the Crown Prince of Dubai, the President of the Prince's Council in Bahrain, and even an Oval Office meeting with President Obama.

Our focus on exports paid off in 2013 when we set a new record, with export sales representing close to forty percent of the company's total volume sales. And by May 2015, we had increased our presence to nearly seventy countries. A major benefit of growing export sales was our ability to increase our workforce and bring back some of the jobs that were lost during the recession.

Over the years Nautique has been the official towboat for a number of international tournaments, including the The Masters, Nautique Asian Championships, Wakeboard Nationals, Wakesurf Worlds, Big Dawg, and the Moomba Masters. We had the privilege to witness incredible international growth in waterskiing, wakeboarding, and wakesurfing. And the developing markets in Asia, South America, and the Middle East were fueling that growth.

Today, Correct Craft sells a large percentage of boats internationally, and I expect that market will continue expanding. We have nearly 100 international dealers in about 70 countries, and we're happy with both our efforts and the results.

■ ■ ■

Another part of the company's long-term plan was to grow and diversify the business by way of acquisitions—inviting others to join our family. In August 2012 we revisited this idea, but instead of approaching boat manufacturers, who weren't yet ready, we purchased the Orlando Watersports Complex (OWC). It was a move that raised some eyebrows at the time, as many marine businesses saw cable parks as competition to boating.

Our team saw just the opposite. Bringing people into watersports by sharing the experience of actually being on the water behind a boat had huge potential for the company. So, for the time being, we directed our attention to cable parks under the umbrella of a new subsidiary—Aktion Parks. The world's most visited wake park, OWC now offers three cable systems combined with a boat lake where riders and skiers can train, and an aquapark for overall family fun. Three years later we opened Miami Watersports Complex (MWC), and in 2019 we opened a third, Elite Cable Park, between Orlando and Tampa. All three parks provide the option to enjoy watersports either on the cable or behind one of our Nautique boats.

As the market improved, additional opportunities presented themselves. And because our owner has been generous with allowing us to keep earnings in the company, we were in a perfect place to help sellers of companies protect their employees, brands, and legacies.

The first acquisition after OWC was Pleasurecraft Engine Group (PEG), manufacturer of four engine brands—PCM Marine Engines, Crusader Engines, Challenger, and Levitator Performance Airboat Engines—which we acquired in October 2014. The addition of PEG was a logical step for several reasons: PEG was a longtime supplier to Nautique, with great brands and a great culture that fit nicely into the Correct Craft family. The primary reason, though, was because the company's owner, Paul Fletcher, was looking for a buyer he trusted to manage his legacy and take care of his employees. All of these factors made PEG an attractive new part of our team.

Our acquisition of freshwater fishing boat brands Bass Cat and Yar-Craft in March 2015 was a similar situation. The Pierce family was looking for someone committed to investing in the companies and being a good steward. They didn't want to sell to a private equity firm that would come in and try to figure out every way to squeeze the employees and vendors. In addition, the opportunity to expand outside the water-sports market made these brands especially attractive. Manufactured in Mountain Home, Arkansas, both Bass Cat (the premier bass fishing boat) and Yar-Craft (the premier walleye fishing boat) are the quality leaders in their segments.

Another factor that supported the acquisition of Bass Cat and Yar-Craft was the superior service they provided. I'd spoken to customers and was impressed with the way they raved about the companies. When I met their teams, I immediately knew they were good people, and that was all we needed to know. We were in, and I was honored they had chosen us.

Then, just three months later in June 2015, Correct Craft acquired Centurion Boats and Supreme Boats. Both brands, powered by Correct Craft's PCM and Crusader Engines, are manufactured in Merced, California. Centurion and Supreme have long and proud histories in the towed watersports segment. Centurion has been the official boat of the World Wake Surfing Championships since they began in 1995. In 2011 Centurion acquired Supreme Boats.

While we could have started another towboat brand, we saw in Centurion and Supreme both brand equity and existing dealer bases that would fit well into the Correct Craft family. As with previous acquisitions, our goal was to share our culture and the way that we operate, and at the same time preserve the unique aspects of their cultures that led to their success.

The following year, in May 2016, we entered the aluminum fishing boat market with the purchase of SeaArk Boats. Manufactured in Monticello, Arkansas, SeaArk is the quality leader in its segment, with both outstanding product and customer service reputations. During its fifty-eight years at the helm of the industry's premier aluminum fishing boat company, the McClendon family succeeded because of its strong brand, great reputation, and exceptional team.

Though it was a bittersweet decision for the family to exit the recreational boating business, they felt they had found the right owner in Correct Craft. Robin McClendon, who believed that the company's team members and legacy were in good hands, said she couldn't be happier to have them joining the Correct Craft family. In turn, we were honored that they would trust their brand to Correct Craft.

Eight months later, in January 2017, we announced that Bryant Boats would be joining the Correct Craft family. A respected, high-quality boat brand that produces stern drive runabouts in Sweetwater, Tennessee, Bryant Boats has been operated by some of the industry's most renowned builders and designers. The company was founded in 1990, continuing a Bryant family tradition of boat building that spanned over fifty years, based on strong Christian principles and American ingenuity.

Knowing our family-oriented culture and our focus on building exceptional products and taking care of customers, the owner was confident that Bryant's heritage would be secure with Correct Craft. In addition, the company would have the resources it needed to grow to a global luxury runabout brand while maintaining its core values.

In April 2019 we entered the offshore boating market with the acquisition of Parker Boats, a fifty-five-year-old company based in Beaufort, North Carolina, that builds offshore and inshore fishing boats. We were thrilled to have Parker Boats join the Correct Craft family. Linwood Parker and his family had built an impressive business and brand with an outstanding team. More importantly, Correct Craft and Parker's values are aligned, which will help us continue to execute our mission of "Building Boats to the Glory of God."

While the purchase allowed us to expand into a new segment of the marine industry, it also gave the Parker team the means to increase its production capacity and bring new product and engineering technologies to the plant, where it manufactures center consoles, sport cabins, walk-arounds, and dual consoles.

That same month we added Velvet Drive Transmissions under the PEG umbrella, following a great forty-year working relationship with the company. Based in Liberty, South Carolina, Velvet Drive has a sixty-five-year reputation for making the highest-quality marine transmissions, V-drives, and industrial equipment in the world. Not only was this a good vertical integration for our engine company, it also provided us with another innovation platform.

The common thread among the boat companies we've acquired so far is that they have great brands, loyal employees, high-quality product, and devoted customers. They also had owners who valued our culture and wanted to sell to someone who would respect and protect what they'd built—and we try hard to be that kind of buyer. Our goal is to ensure that their companies, legacies, and employees continue to thrive well into the future.

A good example of how this plays out was the completion of a significant expansion at SeaArk's Arkansas plant. When we bought the company, they had a six-month order backlog. It turned out they had great product, but not the production capacity to deliver. After we made some targeted capital investments and improved their manufacturing flow through the implementation of Lean Six Sigma processes, the plant was able to accommodate growing sales demand well into the future.

■ ■ ■

Correct Craft has grown significantly in recent years. We now have close to 1,700 employees across the country, and the company generated about $600 million in sales in 2019. Much of this growth was the result of optimization, market expansion, and acquisitions, but our most exciting growth area has been the creation of *new* technologies—otherwise known as innovation through "disruptive" technology. This is the fourth leg of our multi-pronged growth strategy for "Building Boats to the Glory of God."

Innovation is a passion of mine. I've always been interested in the future and what it will bring. To that end, a couple years ago I attended a six-day program at Singularity University, which had many of the world's top technology experts sharing their thoughts on where technology is going and how it will impact the world. Following that course, I became more convinced than ever that the world will be dramatically different in ten years.

In fact, I believe the world will be *so* different that many of the companies we know today, including those in the boating industry, will be at risk for survival. With this in mind, I wanted to redouble Correct Craft's efforts and focus on disruptive innovations. To do that, we invested millions of dollars to create a new entity solely devoted to innovation.

In February 2018 we set up Watershed Innovation as a separate company under Correct Craft. Its mission is to focus on disruptive technologies while the existing brands continue to improve product lines. Watershed's goals are to identify, research, develop, and integrate exponential technologies to benefit Correct Craft, its subsidiaries, the entire marine industry, and, ultimately, the boating public.

Since Watershed's creation, several companies have been added under that umbrella. The first, in July 2018, was Ingenity, which started as a way for a European dealer to sell boats into markets with environmental restrictions on gas-powered boats. Under Watershed, Ingenity's technology was quickly improved, including development of a new and unique battery. These changes were implemented into the most advanced watersports boat in the world, the Nautique GS22E. In 2020, Ingenity had its first GS22E retail sales in both the U.S. and Europe.

With the "internet of things" growing quickly, from the beginning Watershed's plans for Ingenity included connectivity. Once the team realized the device used to facilitate connecting electric boats applied equally well to gas boats, Osmosis was born. Osmosis is a connectivity platform that layers legal, analytics, mobile, and cloud-based services on the vast amounts of data produced by a modern boat. With custom branding like the MyNautique app, Osmosis provides information that allows marine OEMs to create better products and experiences for their end customers. The underlying data provides a foundation for future "big data" initiatives, including machine learning and artificial intelligence.

In May 2019, Watershed acquired Merritt Precision, a longtime supplier that manufactures sophisticated, large-format plugs for the marine, automotive, and aerospace industries. Under Watershed, Merritt Precision has significantly increased its milling capacity and expanded to provide other services, including tooling and 3D scanning. With the addition of a new facility in Tennessee, Merritt Precision provides a platform for Correct Craft's expansion into robotics, additive manufacturing, and other innovation initiatives.

With such advances in technology, we believe many companies in our industry will be out of business in ten years. We don't plan to be one of them. We also want to be the clear leader in developing these innovations. I'll go more in depth on disruptive innovation and its far-reaching potential when I talk about the second "P" (performance) in a later chapter.

■ ■ ■

I've been talking a lot about *what* we do as a company, but just as important is *why* we do it. Our *Why*—"Making Life Better"—is all about people and using our resources to make the world better. This conviction influences everything we do.

At Correct Craft, we want to make life better for our customers, our employees and their families, our dealers, vendors and shareholders, our communities, and people from around the world who benefit from our philanthropy. Of course, we also want to be profitable, but we firmly believe there's nothing inconsistent with being both a high-performance organization and having a culture that makes life better for people.

This unwavering focus on using our resources to make the world better, and make life better, is what drives Correct Craft today. It's *why* we do what we do.

When people ask about my proudest accomplishment at Correct Craft, they're sometimes surprised by my response. It has more to do with how many employees are earning certifications and finishing college degrees, with company support, than market-share gains or increased profitability. And when I walk through the facilities of every one of the companies we've acquired, employees thank me for the changes Correct Craft has brought to their company. For me, "Making Life Better" is far more than a feel-good slogan—it's a culture we've instilled across the organization.

I'm thrilled with the cultural improvements we've implemented at Correct Craft. While we want to grow and thrive, it's equally important to us that we treat people well and develop leaders who understand what it means to make life better for others.

Whether it's building a home with Habitat for Humanity here in the U.S., or serving those who need help in far-flung locations around the world, our team is not only committed to building the world's best boats and engines, but also helping to make the world better. I'm proud to be part of this amazing group of people!

■ ■ ■

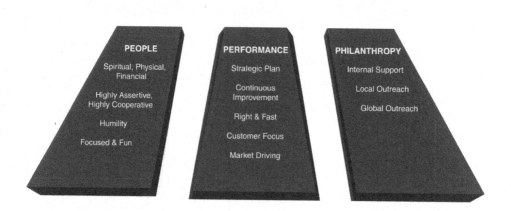

Correct Craft approaches culture in a unique way—by putting others first and caring for the betterment of people. We achieve our goal of "Making Life Better" by prioritizing *People*, *Performance*, and *Philanthropy* in everything we do. These three pillars, also known as *the 3 P's*, are *how* we make life better.

At Correct Craft, our culture drives who we are, and the Identity Pyramid illustrates our most important values. The next three chapters are devoted to these supporting pillars.

■ ■ ■

Final Thoughts

Navigating through the Great Recession was excruciatingly difficult for our team; however, that challenging time helped us lay a great foundation for the record-breaking decade that followed.

After the Great Recession, our excellent team was battle-tested and ready to grow. In subsequent years we totally changed the way we approached global markets, which significantly increased our international sales and profits. We were also able to leverage what we learned to make acquisitions that helped position Correct Craft as a leader in the marine industry.

Finally, and most importantly, it helped us crystalize our thinking regarding who we wanted to be and why we existed. We want to build great boats and we want to make money, but more importantly, we want to Make Life Better. We want to have a positive impact on everyone we meet and use our platform for good. We captured that in our Identity Pyramid, and I deeply appreciate how our team has embraced its concepts.

9

IDENTITY PYRAMID – PEOPLE

One of the key factors driving Correct Craft's success has been our company culture. "Making Life Better" is not just a tagline—it's our core philosophy. The best companies are intentional about their culture. They have to know why they exist; that's why "Making Life Better" is so important to us.

It's no surprise that the first pillar supporting our "Why" of making life better is People. The first pillar represents "How" we serve our employees and their families. This pillar incorporates everything from pay, benefits, good working conditions, and a great culture, to improving our employees' relationships by energizing and caring for their loved ones. We provide all the typical benefits you would expect from a company our size, but also try to go beyond the expected.

Because every organization is unique, when a new company joins the Correct Craft family, we work hard to preserve their culture and what's made *them* successful, while at the same time sharing ours. When new team members see a company that truly cares for them, they in turn feel better about their daily lives.

■ ■ ■

Spiritual, Physical, Financial. These three priorities top our list of values under the first pillar, People. Because we want our employees to be well rounded, we invest in them spiritually, physically, and financially. Our employees have the opportunity to take advantage of a wide range of benefits, such as Bible studies, tuition reimbursement and loan programs, scholarship programs for their children, on-site fitness centers, continuing education, leadership courses, and a mentorship program. We often provide a company match when employees hold fundraisers to support one another.

Across the organization, each Correct Craft company holds special events that run the gamut from employee and vendor appreciation days, Manufacturing Day, holiday parties and monthly BBQ Fridays, to quarterly luncheons and fishing tournaments.

Another key part of our philosophy is to share financial success with our employees, and not just those at the top. We currently have nearly 1,700 people working at Correct Craft, and almost all of them are eligible for bonuses if their team succeeds. I love sharing our success with those who help make it happen.

The returns run far and wide, from spiritual development, culture development, buy-in, and employee retention, to the growth of key relationships. Investing heavily in employee development also enables Correct Craft to attract new employees through referrals. Our platform gives us multiple opportunities to make life better, and that motivates me.

Highly Assertive, Highly Cooperative. In other words, "No Silent Liars." To that end, we've worked hard to foster a unique, high-trust culture that encourages open communication and different perspectives. As a result, politics are almost non-existent, and the group puts the team, our products, and brands above the individual.

In order to make life better, we know we need a culture of excellence that values everyone in the organization and seeks input from each team member. We still have high expectations and hold people accountable for their results, but they are much more likely to want to produce in the right environment, knowing their input matters to their leaders.

We also know that not every idea is always the best idea, so it's important to have a variety of perspectives. For this to happen, employees must feel that they can be open and honest. Over the years I've found that this highly assertive, highly cooperative environment encourages people to speak up and share ideas to make our company better.

Humility. We want to remain humble. There's a great book called *Derailed* that talks about the fall of CEOs who thought they knew best because they'd had so much previous success. I believe the most effective company cultures are humble and high trust/high care.

I learned long ago that the best way to be successful is to surround myself with people smarter than me, and I feel that I've done that at Correct Craft. Our company presidents and Correct Craft team are incredible. They fully embrace our culture, and get impressive results.

Focused & Fun. We want our employees to be focused, but also have fun and enjoy coming to work every day. At Correct Craft, working hard and playing hard produces an incredibly productive and "can-do" culture that makes the days go fast and working fun.

■ ■ ■

Employee development has always been a Correct Craft priority, but in recent years it has taken center stage. The company has invested countless hours and dollars in professional and personal growth, and continuous learning for all of our teams across the country. We want well-rounded personnel.

When I joined Correct Craft, one of my priorities was to offer employees a variety of opportunities to continue their education, both formally and informally. Continuous improvement is a key part of our culture—and it's not just limited to technology. We talk a lot about our desire to be "learners, not knowers." There's no way we could have accomplished what our team has been able to do as *knowers*, and I'm happy that so many at Correct Craft and our companies aspire to be *learners*.

One of the ways we've done this is by adopting a reading culture. Reading plays a key role in our focus on continuous improvement, and we build it into our training. At any given time multiple team members are working through a book. I'll often recommend one if I think it will help. It's what our team calls "getting booked!"

For several years, we held a monthly staff book club. Each month one employee selected a book for the club to read and then discuss what they've learned. The book club added value by improving communication and helping people understand how others process information. For example, it allows an engineer to see firsthand how a person in marketing or in operations interprets the concepts of a given book. This was a great team asset.

I love to read and I finish dozens of books a year. While I enjoy sharing book recommendations, and receiving them as well, there is no way I could list the hundreds of books that have influenced me over the years. But here are a few I consider "must reads" for our business leaders and anyone interested in personal development:

The Seven Habits of Highly Effective People by Stephen Covey is a classic I've read and taught numerous times. Simon Sinek's *Start with Why* is a powerful read that set the tone for Correct Craft when we began expanding several years ago. *Six Thinking Hats* by Dr. Edward de Bono explains why we get trapped in our way of viewing things, and provides a great tool for expanding our teams' thinking. *The Five Dysfunctions of a Team* by Patrick Lencioni, which describes the many pitfalls teams face as they seek to grow together. *Being Wrong* by Kathryn Schulz and *The Truth About Us* by Brant Hansen both explore what it means to be in error, and finally there's *How to Win Friends and Influence People* by Dale Carnegie, a classic on how to deal with others. (You've just been "booked"!)

Our guest speaker series is another popular initiative that has kept employees learning. This ongoing program brings authors, athletes, business leaders, and other inspirational speakers to the company with the goal of both spiritual and professional development. For example, early last year Jack Barsky, former Soviet KGB agent and author of the book *Deep Undercover: My Secret Life and Tangled Allegiances as a KGB Spy in America*, visited the Correct Craft and Nautique Boats Orlando facility and spoke at an all-employee meeting about his experiences. Barsky shared spy stories and discussed his post-Cold War transformation to a U.S. citizen.

As a surprise guest, we welcomed back Michele Rigby Assad during Barsky's visit. Assad, an ex-CIA agent who authored the book *Breaking Cover: My Secret Life in the CIA and What It Taught Me about What's Worth Fighting For,* had previously spoken to the group. It was a fun and unique experience to have both authors at the factory together. The team enjoyed hearing Jack Barsky speak and seeing Michele Assad again. They both have interesting, compelling, and inspirational stories.

Brant Hansen, author of *Unoffendable, Blessed Are the Misfits,* and *The Truth About Us*, is another team favorite. Other speakers have included Franklin Graham, Truett Cathy, and professional golfer Bubba Watson.

Correct Craft has always promoted continuing education. We have many employees who've gone back to school to earn certifications, including black belts in Lean Six Sigma, and many who have returned to earn graduate degrees. When I arrived at Correct Craft, I'm pretty sure I was the first MBA in the company's history. Since then, through our support, almost thirty of our employees have gone back to college and earned MBAs.

The flip side of formal degrees and certifications at our company is the mentorship program. Angela Pilkington, who began her Correct Craft career in 1981 as a temporary employee, is one of its strongest advocates. She worked her way up to administrative assistant and then held multiple roles—including her current position as Correct Craft's executive vice president/chief of staff—while raising a family and completing two degrees. Angela has been a leader, mentor, and coach at all different levels as she's grown with the company. In her current role, Angela works with our subsidiaries to drive initiatives and execute strategic plans at each company, while mentoring female employees across the organization.

Few things provide me as much satisfaction as developing our people. And one of the greatest benefits of our expansion has been that it provides opportunities for many on our team to learn new things and grow into new roles. That excites me!

Our growth through acquisitions also provided the impetus for us to create Correct Craft University (CCU) in January 2019. An important next step in our learning culture, it's designed to provide every one of our employees across the country a chance to develop their skills. CCU is a voluntary program that provides a variety of opportunities. The personal growth sector focuses on financial management, language, and computer classes. Professional growth concentrates on on-the-job training skills. And CCU also offers a leadership course that reinforces existing skills and prepares individuals with the expertise they need to advance.

We tailor these courses specifically to each Correct Craft brand. Education and development take place in several formats: on-site training classes, individual micro-learning videos, webinars, and assigned readings. A book club and cross-functional team meetings are facilitated at each company to bring staff together and build individual acumen and team comradery. Best of all, employees completing the program are eligible to apply for promotional opportunities within the entire Correct Craft organization.

Correct Craft University is equipping our employees to be future leaders at a Correct Craft company or any other place they may work in the future. I'm thrilled about the desire our team has demonstrated to grow and improve.

■ ■ ■

Many of our company presidents have seen dramatic changes since their organization joined Correct Craft, and I couldn't be happier with the impact our "Making Life Better" culture has had on their people.

One of them is Paul Singer, president of Centurion and Supreme. According to Paul, when Correct Craft purchased the brands there was distrust between the employees and management.

"Most of this stemmed from miscommunication and lack of clarity for the employees, resulting in poor quality and output," he explained. "In the end, no investment was more important to creating change in the critical areas of the business than earning back that trust and developing a strong culture within the organization."

When Paul, already an industry legend, took the president's position with the company, he knew that a third of the employees would probably follow him, another third would wait and see, and another third would resist anything he proposed. "I found that we really accelerated that middle sector of employees by giving to them without expecting a return right from the start. Employees began to see the changes. Attitudes started to transform, and we introduced a 'Why' into the factory. That 'why' of Making Life Better included their own, and they liked that."

Paul and other leaders became intentional with more frequent communication, employee praise, and vision-casting. Their teams believed that getting a bonus was possible, and that this new employer followed through with their promises.

"We started holding quarterly plant meetings and updating employees on important areas of the business, including their financial performance. I let them know exactly where we were at and that employee incentives existed for those companies whose performance exceeded reasonable financial returns. A profit of ten percent of sales became the mantra of sorts at factory meetings. I would ask 'Where do we need to be?' and they would shout back 'ten percent!'"

These changes brought a dramatic response.

"Employee participation levels in company service projects began to go up, and there was more communication on the floor. In time, employees started helping each other finish their jobs—whereas before, when one department would finish they would just go home or, even worse, stand around. Attitudes among the employees were changing."

Paul shared that his leaders made the decision to invest in their employees before the financial results made sense. They provided health insurance and a 401k plan, and began giving reasonable raises to employees, some of whom hadn't seen a raise in years. "We created employee break areas, installed ice machines, and made plant safety a priority. We recognized employee anniversaries and started a voluntary Bible Study Lunch, then a second Women's Bible Study Lunch, and then a third Spanish-speaking Bible Study Lunch. These lunches are supplied free of charge to anyone who attends."

Today at Centurion and Supreme, it's all about *people*. Paul takes great pride in the humility, encouragement, and perseverance now being demonstrated by his team. "They don't care who gets the credit, yet they are a key component of that victory. They enjoy winning together and celebrating each other's victories. And they often say 'Failure is not an option. Let's go do this!'" He also enjoys watching new leaders and employees step up and out of their comfort zones, assuming leadership roles and implementing new standards and processes.

According to Paul, Centurion and Supreme have undergone a remarkable cultural transformation. "When we had our first Open House and BBQ for employee families, you could see the incredible pride that their spouses and children showed as our team members explained what they did to create these magnificent boats! Correct Craft has made lives better in Merced, California."

There have been spectacular results in all areas of Centurion and Supreme. I have known many great leaders, but of all of them, Paul may be the most impactful.

Steve Henderson, president of SeaArk, has also seen many beneficial changes since his company became part of the Correct Craft family. He enjoys sharing the different ways our philosophy helps make life better for his team in Monticello, Arkansas.

"Since the acquisition there's been a big improvement in the way employees treat one another. I attribute this to our team members having a better work environment," Steve observed. "We recently upgraded several areas of the facility, including repairing roofs, supplying proper tools, and adding fans and heaters. Plus, we improved the lunchroom with healthier options like salads, instead of junk food."

These steps, along with Bible study, quarterly luncheons, and events such as their employee picnic/fishing tournament, have helped increase production, which in turn allowed them to improve overall salaries throughout the plant. "There's also a bonus program in place that includes both skilled and unskilled labor," Steve noted.

"Having a faith-based foundation is one of the things that makes me happy to be part of the Correct Craft team. The thing I'm most proud of is the night one of our team members gave his life to the Lord in Bible study. Ultimately, that is what it's all about. This was a direct result of the company's faith-based culture—not only making life better, but making the afterlife better."

Steve believes that Correct Craft University and the mentorship program also show team members that the company cares for them, helping train future "want to be" leaders and allowing every team member advancement opportunities. At SeaArk, the mentorship program assigns seasoned employees to new hires to help them adjust to the workplace. "It helps improve culture by making them feel a part of the team right from the beginning. Since we began these programs, just hearing the positive feedback and responses to the questionnaires is awesome," Steve explained.

■ ■ ■

Last summer, after interviewing some of our team members around the country, one of our industry's publications, *Trade Only Today*, published an article on Correct Craft's unique culture. Their stories clearly echo the words of their company leaders. The growth these employees have experienced as part of the Correct Craft family is a great example of how our values positively impact a business. I found their feedback to be reaffirming and was given the go-ahead to share it here.

Stuart Malone, a thirty-year Bass Cat and Yar-Craft employee, said he loves that every person is in it for the success of one another and the success of the company as a Correct Craft brand. "I'm still amazed at the family atmosphere," Stuart said. "Everyone's attitude to jump in and get the job done is unique. We have an invitational every year, and seeing people's faces when they experience our heart of service, from parking cars to carrying fish, gives you a sense of pride in what you are doing."

Tino Lucio has worked for Centurion and Supreme for thirty-nine years. He believes that teamwork is when you build confidence among one another and get to know people and what they do. "I'm glad to be around good people who have workmanship, talent, and attitude," Tino shared. "Our team in production is so proud of what we are building. Part of that is because we hear from other departments on some of the successes they have, like boat shows and events. We talk about culture every week, and we stay encouraged by our incredible president, Paul Singer."

Bill Waits is in his forty-fifth year at Nautique and spoke about how Correct Craft's executive team creates an environment of treating others with respect, even in a high-paced, lean manufacturing environment, because they work toward equipping others.

"The politics and interdepartment squabbling are almost nonexistent," Bill said. "We work towards one common goal. It is incredible being a small part of something so large and good for the world. A lot of times you look at politics or bad relationships between companies, but Correct Craft is outstanding and is what I think a company should be."

Jakub Pilecky has been at Orlando Watersports Complex since 2001. He is a watersports expert and enjoys raising a new generation of riders, because he believes it has a huge impact.

"I started with coaching and running the cables, now I really enjoy passing my knowledge to new employees," Jakub said. "I do my best to make sure existing riders are continuing to have a good time, while spreading the sport as far as I can reach. Right now mentoring employees is so vital, because I want them to take something they've learned here to wherever they go next. We are all friends and I care about them on a personal level."

Angela Naron from SeaArk Boats is proud of the good employee turnout for Correct Craft's company-wide service trips, and enjoys the comradery SeaArk has at its optional weekly Bible studies.

"Most of us step up and do above and beyond what is needed, and that's why we love serving others," Angela said. "We always have a good crowd at Bible study. I feel whoever leads helps us dig in and challenges us to do things we hadn't thought about doing before."

Pleasurecraft Engine Group's thirty-four-year employee, Roy Layton, said Correct Craft has made his life better by influencing him to read more often. Roy was always interested in creating a relationship with Nautique leaders, even before Nautique and PCM became sister companies. He wanted to understand what Nautique leaders were talking about, so a Nautique manager gave Layton lists of books Nautique employees were reading. That's when he started listening to books.

"It goes back to inspiration," Roy explained. "I never liked reading, but in this case, Nautique was influential in making me better, even before PCM became a part of the Correct Craft family. Today, our CEO, Bill Yeargin, is very generous in a way that I can email him anytime, and he will give suggestions on books I would like."

Tommy Ferguson, who has been with Bryant Boats (now Correct Craft Tennessee) since 1988, is a big fan of the company and its learning culture. "Ever since Correct Craft, we are stocked with new tools and new equipment," Tommy said. "It is really exciting to build now. We were used to doing all the maintenance with either old tools or simply by hand. My team has been together so long, and we work well together. The entire crew is excited—there's a lot of opportunity to grow with Correct Craft University. CCU is helping us develop as leaders. I love that it opens my mind for new ideas to kick-start and help me be a more effective leader."

■ ■ ■

At Correct Craft, we see culture not as an expense but as an investment, with a huge return that can't be measured in dollars. It's simple, really— when you build your people, you build your business.

In fact, our belief in the importance of our values and culture is so strong that we hosted the boating industry's first annual Culture Summit in early 2020, underwriting all costs of the conference. Our goal was to share the benefits of being a culture-driven company, and to learn from other marine industry executives and HR professionals.

The Culture Summit, which explored the importance of effective culture in our companies, included workshops to help attendees identify key aspects of an effective culture and create an implementation plan for their companies. Industry leaders from Grady White, Regal, Correct Craft, and others spoke about how culture transformed their businesses to the benefit of those both in and outside their organizations. The event also had two special guest speakers: Brant Hansen, author of *Unoffendable*, and Dr. Wallace J. Nichols, author of *Blue Mind*.

I said this multiple times during the two-day summit, but it's worth repeating: Culture drives results. Our Correct Craft team has seen first-hand the power of an effective culture. It has been critical to the growth of our company, and we're determined to do what we can to share with others, including competitors, the powerful ideas and principles that we've learned. It's about people, the power of culture, and its ability to transform.

■ ■ ■

Final Thoughts

It has been exciting to see how a company culture can drive results. Not just financial results, but cultural and eternal results. For us, culture has not been a cost, but rather an investment with a huge return. We are thrilled with how our culture impacts people both inside and outside our company.

It is also important for us to invest in our people. We encourage them to be "learners," and I appreciate how that idea has been integrated into the lives of our teams.

10
IDENTITY PYRAMID – PERFORMANCE

The second of the three pillars supporting our "Why" of making life better is Performance. It embodies all of the ways we make life better by making what we *have* better—from the products we build and the service we provide, to the memorable experiences we help create every day.

But this pillar doesn't stand alone. Each of our pyramid's three pillars depends and builds upon the other. For example, our "People" culture is Correct Craft's number one driver of results. In other words, because of our employees, we're able to provide our customers with great product, service, and experiences. In turn, exceptional "Performance" allows us to use the proceeds of those sales to make the world better through "Philanthropy," which further energizes our employees.

With the resources we generate by being profitable, we're able to give and to serve. In the end, a company's culture and the ways it maximizes revenue—through creativity, innovation, quality products and services, a strong margin, and good customer relationships—are the main drivers that make it all happen.

But we don't do this alone. Under the second pillar there's a wide-ranging cast of players that we strive to serve and who, in turn, help us make what we have better. Over the years our suppliers and dealers, our industry as a whole, our shareholder, and our customers have all helped us create and shape what "Making Life Better" is about.

Correct Craft is most fortunate to have outstanding vendors and dealers. They provide great product and support, and we love to both show our thanks and nurture these relationships. For example, our companies host Vendor Appreciation Days to let their supplier partners know how much we appreciate their partnership. We also hold annual dealer meetings and work closely with their dealerships throughout the year to help us keep customer satisfaction high. I enjoy hearing from vendors and dealers at these events who tell me of the noticeable difference in our culture.

We're also active in advocating for the recreational marine industry by supporting key organizations, such as the Water Sports Industry Association (WSIA), and by partnering with the American Boating Association (ABA) and National Marine Manufacturers Association (NMMA). For several years, we've also been a big proponent of National

Manufacturing Day. All of our companies host an annual open house for high school and college students to help promote manufacturing as a desirable career.

Of course, much of our focus is on our customers and their families, who value performance over all else. Each and every day, Correct Craft companies work constantly to cultivate their customer relationships by providing superior product, service, and experiences, and strive to make what we have *even better* through continuous improvement and market-driving innovation.

■ ■ ■

The second pillar represents "How" we serve our various partners and stakeholders through Performance, along with the five values that drive us.

Strategic Plan - We are a strategic plan-driven company that highly values its culture. That's why we heavily focus on maintaining a highly relational culture. Our strategic planning process emphases on the three pillars of our Identity Pyramid, which captures both what is important to us and how we want to conduct ourselves. Even more important than doing things right is identifying what the right things are. To me, that is the beauty of a strategic plan.

Continuous Improvement - We are a continuous improvement company. Correct Craft University is one of the many ways we achieve this goal. We believe there's always room for improvement, and will never stop looking for ways to get better. We know that when we do this, it benefits our customers. *That* is what makes us happy.

Right & Fast - We strive to be both right and fast. You don't want to be wrong and fast—that will put you out of business. You don't want to be right and slow, because you will miss opportunities and get left behind. Maintaining a balance is the key. At Correct Craft, we've created a business model that enables us to be fast out the door with exciting new product, while also being able to ensure that it's done right, and it meets our exacting standards.

Customer Focus - We are a customer-focused company. We're here to serve our customers with products that they enjoy and are proud to own, always exceeding expectations by providing the best possible service and experiences.

Market Driving - Most companies want to be market driven, but we strive to be a market-driving company, the leader of our industry. In addition to being responsive to what our customers and dealers tell us, we want to give the marketplace something they've never thought of before and *make what we have better,* in a more dramatic way.

■ ■ ■

Correct Craft's dedication to the values of continuous improvement and customer focus are two key areas that set us apart from others in our industry. Our product development teams are incredible, and they all live the boating life. They're always on the water, either skiing, wakeboarding, wakeskating, wakesurfing, or fishing, and they know what people want.

Taking that a step further, each one of our brands shares an insatiable drive to ensure they have the industry's best product. They're practically obsessed with innovation and creating the best products on the market, all with the same goal in mind: making life better by making what we have better.

In addition, these companies demonstrate a commitment to customer service that might not make sense to others. We make decisions all the time that may not be the best short-term decisions but the right decision for the long term. I would much rather build brand loyalty than have short-term profits, and I believe this attitude sets a company apart for long-term success.

■ ■ ■

Correct Craft strives to be the industry-driving company, staying at the forefront of innovation and challenging ourselves to create something better that improves our customers' ownership experience. Each year we continue to revolutionize the industry with cutting-edge products, working side by side with our dealers and vendors.

Our focus on continuous improvement started paying off big in 2015 with a series of highly successful product launches. In July of that year, amid celebrations in honor of its ninetieth anniversary, Nautique announced the next evolution of its award-winning G-Series boats—the *2016 Super Air Nautique G23 and G25*. These new boats featured ground-breaking advancements, including a new hull and interior design, as well as advances in technology, such as the all-new Nautique Surf Select, a remote wave customization system controlled by the surfer from behind the boat. The following spring, the Super Air Nautique G23 received the WSIA (Water Sports Industry Association) Leadership Award for Most Innovative Product of the Year. A year later, it was honored during the WakeWorld Riders Choice Awards for both Wakeboarding Boat of the Year and Wakesurfing Boat of the Year for 2017. Since then, it has received the Wakesurf award five more times, and the Wakeboard award a total of seven years, the longest-standing consecutive wins.

In August 2015, Centurion announced an equally exciting new product release, the *2016 Ri237*. The next level in World Championship Towboat performance, design, and craftsmanship, the Ri237 featured a newly designed Deep-V Hull, seamless integration of Centurion's signature wake enhancement technology, an exotic sports car exterior, and its patented Side-by-Side High Definition (SxS HD) Touch Vision technology, which improved driver control of World Championship Centurion boats, as well as the look of the dash. The year following its launch, the 2017 Ri237 was named a Boating Industry 2017 Top Product. It was selected from hundreds of new or updated products for its innovation, impact on the industry, and creativity.

This was followed a month later by Pleasurecraft Engine Group when it announced a new portfolio of watersports engines featuring direct injection technology—the only direct injection engines at that time offered in the inboard market. These innovative *HYPERFORMANCE H5DI and H6DI* models featured new, industry-leading horsepower and torque—creating outstanding performance—and were the most fuel-efficient engines in their class.

The following year, our Supreme brand announced its *2017 Supreme S202* towboat, which was completely created through a vacuum infusion process (VIP). This included all composite components of the boats, including plugs and molds. The technology created a stronger, more consistent boat, while drastically reducing emissions.

By the spring of 2017, the engineering team at Centurion and Supreme Boats had made some great discoveries, and there would be many more innovations to come. Over the previous twelve months Centurion and Supreme Boats had combined to become the fastest growing towboat brands in the industry, showing nearly eighty percent growth compared with the prior year's retail registrations.

We were definitely on a roll—but the product enhancements and innovations didn't end there. In May 2018, Nautique announced the introduction of the all new Ski Nautique. For nearly sixty years, the Ski Nautique had been the best waterski boat in the world. Those blood-lines continued with the radically improved *2019 Ski Nautique*, which was reinvented as the lightest three-event towboat on the market. With a blended carbon fiber and fiberglass construction, this new-generation Ski Nautique was destined to become the standard in tournament waterski towboats.

Less than a year later at the NMMA Innovation Awards, Nautique took home the Propulsion Equipment and Parts Award for *MicroTuner* technology that was incorporated into the 2019 Ski Nautique. The MicroTuners deploy from the transom of the Ski Nautique and cause a disturbance in the water that fills in the troughs of the wake, providing the waterskier a superior experience. This technology had previously never been done, and the patented MicroTuners were credited as one of the most significant waterskiing innovations in recent years .

Then, in March 2019, the WSIA presented Supreme Boats with a Watersports Innovation Award for its *ZS Series Tapered-V Hull*. Developed to displace more water with less ballast weight, the Tapered-V hull offered an extremely long surf wave that can be achieved quickly and last all day. Creating a smooth rough-water ride with double the degree of V (deadrise) as competitors, it proved that premium performance can be built into a value-class towboat. In July 2019, the Supreme Boats ZS series was also featured as one of Boating Industry's sixth annual "Top Products" for 2018.

One of Correct Craft's highest honors was being recognized out of 35,000 marine companies as the "Most Innovative Company" in the industry by *Soundings Trade Only* magazine in October of 2019 and then once again in 2020. This award recognizes all of our companies for their innovative technologies, culture, learning environment, and M&A strategy.

When *Wakeboarding Magazine* released their 2019 Reader's Poll in December 2019, we were honored that *two* of our towboats achieved top-five placements in the "Favorite Boat Brand" category. Nautique was ranked number one by voters, solidifying its position as the most aspired top brand in towed watersports. Centurion Boats clocked in at position number four. The Centurion brand has experienced immense success in the last few years with the Ri237 serving as the official tow-boat of the 2019 World Wake Surfing Championship as well as the 2019 IWWF World Wakeboard Championships. These awards were proof of our team's commitment to crafting compelling products that exceed expectations, while growing the love of our top brands with riders from around the globe.

Bass Cat and Yar-Craft Boats also have continued to excel with fresh innovations as they strive to remain at the top of their industry. Coming out of its fiftieth year, in January 2020 Yar-Craft received top honors in the fiberglass fishing boats category for its 219 TFX at the Minneapolis Boat Show. Drawing on the culture and roots they are known for in bass boats, Yar-Craft created a new platform in the multi-species world by bringing together unique design improvements and quality manufacturing elements.

Then, four months later, Yar-Craft's flagship model was named one of *Boating Industry Magazine's* 2020 Top Products. Completely redesigned internal assemblies, including an all-fiberglass transom that extends the entire width of the boat, along with a full-featured deck to serve a variety of anglers' needs, were key details that caught the attention of one of the boating industry's premier media companies.

To cap it all off, the 2020 Miami International Boat Show's product innovation awards event was one of the most gratifying I've ever attended. Correct Craft's brands were presented with multiple innovation awards spanning several categories at the National Marine Manufacturers Association annual awards breakfast. Judged by the Boating Writers International, the Innovation Award is the recreational boating industry's highest honor for innovative and technological achievement.

The highlight of the morning was during the NMMA Innovation Awards ceremony where Nautique's G23 Paragon was awarded one of the marine industry's highest achievements for product innovation. In the Towboat category, the Super Air Nautique G23 Paragon took home this coveted Innovation Award for its overall innovation. Introduced with critical acclaim in October 2019, the industry's first luxury performance wake boat was styled with prestigious craftsmanship that cultivates the best-performing wakeboarding and wakesurfing waves. The G23 Paragon delivers unparalleled performance, with a host of innovative features like a telescoping tower, hull-sides used as a running surface, and the ability to literally dial in the ideal surf wake. At the show, in partnership with Ingenity, our electric propulsion brand, Nautique also debuted the first electric Super Air Nautique GS22E. As part of this debut, the Miami International Boat Show awarded Ingenity the Miami International Boat Show Innovation Award for its electric drive system.

In addition, Pleasurecraft Engine Group received the Innovation Award in the Inboard Engine category for its entirely new PCM Z Series of engines—the most comprehensive product portfolio of engines in the inboard industry, spanning five engine models, ranging from 400HP-600HP. With catalytic converters, closed cooling, and the ability to run on 89 octane, Pleasurecraft Marine's (PCM) Z series engines are environmentally friendly and provide a wide range of power options. And PCM's Service Focused Design was a leading concept in the development of the Z Series, mandating common service points across multiple engine designs. The engineering team spent thousands of hours designing, developing, and validating this entirely new portfolio of engines. It was no easy feat, and we were grateful to receive this industry recognition.

■ ■ ■

The desire to exceed our customers' expectations through continuous improvement, innovative products, and the boating experiences they're craving drives every Correct Craft company and employee. But customer focus is about more than product and performance. Our job isn't complete without a commitment to great customer service, both before and after the sale, and an ownership experience people can feel good about. The other half of our "customer focus" is providing the service and support they need, as well as user experiences that enhance their ownership.

This passion for customer satisfaction is what drives us to always exceed expectations by providing the best possible service and experiences, and that starts by creating a better buying experience. One of my favorite examples is the online boat building feature several of our manufacturers offer.

Nautique received runner-up honors during the NMMA's 2020 Neptune Awards ceremony for its web site, which features an enhanced "Design Your Nautique" interactive boat builder, unique podcasts, and a responsive site design that's available in five languages. The helpful boat-building tool lets viewers envision their perfect boat by selecting every aspect of their ideal model, design, and configuration.

Sometimes, our unrelenting commitment to service and helping our owners enjoy their time on the water means going above and beyond. I see this all around me every day. Mark McKinney, Pleasurecraft Engine Group president, shared a story that illustrates the kinds of people who have made Correct Craft what we are today.

"We consistently receive accolades from customers and dealers saying they wouldn't use any other brand. One example of this unsolicited praise is a letter I received from a customer applauding two of our employees who went out of their way, on their own time, to fix his boat and save his weekend with his family," Mark shared. "During the buying experience the dealer had been very complimentary of PCM and shared some examples of our employees who had even helped customers on the water. While he appreciated the stories, the owner figured it was just part of the hype."

That summer, the owner was out on the water on a Friday afternoon when his boat threw a belt. The dealer wouldn't be able to look at it until the next day. Unfortunately, he had family arriving from out of town the next day for a big boating event and knew there was no way he'd be back on the water in time.

"After he and his daughter sat stranded for an hour or so, one of our employees who happened to live on the lake, Patrick Amann, towed the owner back to his own house and said to leave it there so he could repair it," recalled Mark. "Patrick then went to the factory for the necessary equipment and drove back with one of our lead technicians to complete the repair. They worked late into the night and kept the owner informed of their progress via text messages, all to ensure that he and his family were able to hit the water Saturday. This owner couldn't have been more effusive in his praise, saying that he was blown away by the level of professionalism and support he received from our team."

■ ■ ■

This kind of selfless dedication to putting our owners first—while also creating products and features they want and enjoy—is the reason Correct Craft companies receive such high praise in the form of the industry's prestigious customer satisfaction awards each year. I was beyond proud when the winners of the 2019 NMMA Marine Industry Customer Satisfaction Index (CSI) Awards were announced this past February at the Miami International Boat Show.

Our teams strive for outstanding customer service, and I was thrilled that the Nautique, Centurion, Supreme, Yar-Craft, and Pleasurecraft teams were all recognized for providing this to their customers. Recipients had to achieve an independently measured standard of excellence of ninety percent or higher for the program year, based on information provided by customers who purchased a new boat or engine during that time frame. The program surveyed 158,335 customers for this reporting period.

The bar for earning this recognition is set quite high. Nine awards were given in the industry's Inboard Watersports Boat segment for 2019 and we took home a third of them. Pleasurecraft was one of only three winners in the Inboard Engine category.

I think Centurion and Supreme president Paul Singer put it best when he said, "Sales success and new product launches are all great, but earning the NMMA CSI Award is the real indicator that our teams are focused on the right things—commitment to product quality and customer service."

Pleasurecraft president Mark McKinney also strongly believes that no company can achieve this kind of recognition from their customers without an incredible team. "Our dealers are also an integral part of our company, and we wouldn't be able to earn these awards without them," he added.

Nautique president Greg Meloon agreed, stating that the CSI Award reflects the dedication of our teams, our suppliers, and our dealer networks. "We're driven to deliver our customers outstanding service and support that starts by delivering the best products available. Our strong partnerships with industry-leading suppliers allow us to introduce products that are innovative, tested, and proven to perform."

I'm truly blessed to work with the best in the business—people who are focused on driving innovation and introducing technology that enriches our customers' experiences on the water. I love our teams!

■ ■ ■

While our boat and engine manufacturing companies have been building new and better products for customers, Watershed Innovation has been "making what we have better" in a more dramatic way. Since its formation in early 2018 to identify, research, develop, and integrate disruptive technologies, Watershed has moved the needle from improving what we already have to introducing entirely *new* technologies to boating. Today, we're not only driving the market—we're giving the market new things they didn't know were possible.

The need for this separate "disruptive" innovation entity became apparent when initiatives like our electric boat venture were falling in between the cracks of the motor company and the boat company. Even though everyone had interest in it, there wasn't enough activity around the project to move it forward. Sometimes the companies involved would want to wrap their arms around it, and at other times they'd want to push it away.

At this point I decided to take a key group of leaders to a week-long Disruptive Innovation class taught by the late Harvard professor Clayton Christensen and his team. The basic theory, explained in his book *The Innovator's Dilemma*, maintains that sustaining and efficiency innovations are in the domain of the existing company. But disruptive innovations are a different animal—they're outside of the structures and resources of that business. So, we established a disruptor, Watershed Innovation, to explore emerging technologies that could transform the industry.

With Watershed Innovation, we were able to create a platform for the people who care about advances like electric propulsion to talk with each other in a more open way, allowing them to make recommendations on strategic direction. We have an interactive forum for those with a passive interest in the projects, but the projects are managed and driven outside of the operating companies.

■ ■ ■

Under the guidance of its president, Sean Marrero, our Watershed Innovation startup began by tapping into the University of Central Florida's honors engineering program to help uncover the best way forward for the industry. Watershed's first project, an ultra-quiet aluminum fishing boat with electric propulsion, involved collaboration with UCF's senior engineering students, our SeaArk aluminum fishing boat company, Torqeedo electric outboards, and SeaDek flooring. This small team looked at all the options out there and recommended we acquire an electric boat drive system, Ingenity P220, which had originated in Austria. This acquisition of the highest-performing electric towboat propulsion system in the world would help prepare our boat brands and Pleasurecraft Engine Group for the inevitable future beyond internal combustion engines.

Each group brought unique capabilities to the table. UCF's team consisted of a dozen senior students from the electrical engineering, mechanical engineering, and computer science departments. They designed the boat we built, including all of the computational fluid dynamics, 3D-printed models to simulate the amount of noise on different shaped designs, and all of the CAD. They also built in their own sensors and PCB board to support a cloud database and mobile app.

Watershed Innovation recruited engineers at SeaArk Boats to actually fabricate the boat and serve as a sounding board for design questions.

This was to ensure that we didn't design a boat that was un-buildable. Supplier SeaDek also provided technical advice and non-skid for further sound reduction, and Torqeedo contributed with electric outboards because we wanted the boat to be fully electric.

The project started in September 2018 and the students had an April 2019 deadline, just a few weeks before finals. They sent all data and files to SeaArk to cut and weld the aluminum boat. When the project was unveiled later that month, it looked unlike a traditional jon boat. Tests showed a thirty percent reduction in the sound of water slapping against the side of the hull versus a jon boat. This helped reduce the noise that's normally experienced with off-shore aluminum boats.

The Watershed Innovation electric towboat was one of 133 senior design projects on display at UCF's 2019 annual showcase. Only Watershed's and one other project were chosen to go to the statewide competition, where Ingenity placed second, behind only NASA! The result of this talented team's work was the world's quietest aluminum bay boat with a specially designed hull and Torqeedo electric power. After the project ended our electric towboat was further improved by Watershed engineers, who increased battery performance and added a sophisticated cooling system.

Today, the Ingenity Electric Drive System is integrated into all Super Air Nautique GS22E models, and the Ingenity high-power electric battery was recognized as an industry game changer twice this year. In February 2020, at the Miami International Boat Show, where they received the Innovation Award in the Electric Motor/Battery Powered Propulsion category, Watershed announced the debut of its Ingenity brand and introduced the new electric drive system. The Ingenity system was praised for going "farther than anyone to date in bringing a high level of electric propulsion to the towboat market."

Then in May, *Boating Industry* magazine named Ingenity a 2020 Top Product. Chosen for its electric drive system powered by a "new and unique" energy-dense battery that fits where a combustion engine is installed, the Ingenity battery allows for two to three hours of typical watersports use, and can be recharged in five hours. And with 200 kW of peak power and near-instantaneous torque, performance is similar to its gas counterpart.

■ ■ ■

From Ingenity more new ideas gained traction and generated additional opportunities for innovation at Watershed, including a startup called Osmosis that does nothing but telematics, or connected boats. Basically, an electric boat is like a floating computer. Because an electric motor has over ninety percent fewer moving parts than a gas motor, not as many things can go wrong and issues are more easily identified. We wanted the ability to monitor those numbers, so we created a device that would remotely send data from the boat to us. And because our gas boat companies had also been looking for a solution to this problem, we adapted the device for them as well.

Through our Osmosis brand the company developed software skills, control software, and analytics, and formed alliances to create systems for connecting and monitoring boats. There is a huge potential for these systems. Time and money is saved when manufacturers can see data from onboard sensors that show a problem emerging before anything goes wrong. It's a win-win for both manufacturers and boat owners.

To demonstrate these possibilities, the Watershed team partnered with Nautique, which has a long-term vision for how telematics can improve the customer experience, and is among the boatbuilders investing in these types of emerging systems. As a result, the marine industry's most advanced telematics system is now standard on all 2020 Nautique models, which are connected to the builder over a cellular network via the MyNautique app.

Our third Watershed Innovation company, Merritt Precision, is an important supplier on the sustaining innovation side that delivers highly sophisticated plugs for the marine, automotive, and aerospace industries. But, in addition to industrial automation, they also give us the ability to work in additive manufacturing, 3D printing, artificial intelligence, robotics, and other disruptive technologies that can become part of the boat building process.

■ ■ ■

We started Watershed Innovation to ideate, iterate, and incubate future technologies for Correct Craft companies and, eventually, the entire marine industry. As the world changes, Correct Craft and Watershed will lead the way due to the work of this innovation center. In 2019 and 2020 *Sounding Trade Only* named us the Most Innovative Marine Company, recognizing our commitment to preparing now for the inevitable and disruptive future."

The magazine's then editor-in-chief, Michael Verdon, stated that what excited him most about his visit to our Orlando headquarters is understanding that innovation can come from such a small group. "Watershed has just ten people working on very different projects. But they are a serious and focused group. If they're an example of what the industry can do, we're in good hands."

Looking ahead to what comes next, I'm reminded of something my youngest daughter once said: "Let's not allow our memories to be bigger than our dreams!" I say, dream on!

■ ■ ■

Final Thoughts

Over the past decade Correct Craft has seen spectacular growth, and we plan to continue growing. This type of growth requires high performance from our team, and we are blessed with a group who embrace that expectation.

We do not want growth for growth's sake, or even for purely financial reasons. We want to build the best products, give the best service, and make money—but we have a higher goal. We know growth will allow us to have a bigger impact and be more effective at "Making Life Better." Growth will allow us to impact more lives for the better in our Correct Craft family, in our communities, and around the world. That excites us!

11

IDENTITY PYRAMID –
PHILANTHROPY

So far, we've talked about the first two pillars of the Correct Craft pyramid and the importance of "People" and "Performance." But it's the third pillar, Philanthropy, that keeps our employees tied to the company's values and rich history. While we want to build the industry's best boats and be profitable, there's something much more meaningful to us: using our resources to make life better for our local communities and people around the world.

The third pillar represents "How" we work to "Make Life Better" through service to others—our own employees, our communities, and our world. We're able to do this by providing customers with great product and using the proceeds of those sales to make lives better for families in need across the globe.

The resources we generate by being profitable make it possible for us to help one another, support our local communities through charitable organizations, and give back to the world through philanthropic work. We do this in a variety of ways.

Internal Support - Our philosophy of service to others begins with the Correct Craft family. We serve employees and provide support and assistance to them in their moments of difficulty. Our companies have had their teams come together to raise money for co-workers with medical needs and donate items when someone lost their house to a fire. It's not unusual for team members to donate vacation time to each other. We want to be there when someone in our Correct Craft circle needs us.

Local Outreach - We want to serve our communities and give back to those less fortunate. Every one of our companies is involved in their local area, helping out with schools and orphanages, cleaning up lakes, building houses for Habitat for Humanity, and donating their time and money to worthy causes. We want to be good partners and make a difference in our communities.

Global Outreach - We also serve globally through service trips and donate our time to make an impact on international communities. In the last thirteen years I've taken employees on trips all over the world—from Cambodia, India, and several countries across Africa, to the Caribbean and Central America. We want to use our resources to help people we will probably never see again, maybe build them a home, make their school better, or work in an orphanage to help someone who's struggling to have a better life.

■ ■ ■

When we started Correct Craft's community and international outreach programs back in 2007, it was part of an effort to begin living out our faith culture less through words and more through actions. The most successful organizations are those with a higher purpose, and we wanted to create a service culture that goes beyond building boats and making money; I wanted us to use our platform and resources to help people who need us.

Giving staff members a chance to take time away from the workplace and focus on a larger cause has made Correct Craft both a better company *and* a better place to work. It lets us step out of our day-to-day functions and help others. There's no question that our philanthropic initiatives have made the company and our teams stronger, while also contributing to the greater good.

Centurion and Supreme Boats have many employees who've welcomed the prospect of giving back. "I'm proud to have the privilege to work for a company that gives me the opportunity to participate in community service days," shared one. "Being part of a team that volunteers gives me a feeling of purpose and enjoyment knowing that I made a difference."

After our first international service trip to Tecate, Mexico, where team members built a house for a homeless family, I asked the group what they thought of the experience. Responses like "the best three days of my life" and "I've never done anything this meaningful" came from all of the employees. I believe it comes down to having something bigger than ourselves to work toward. Since that first trip in 2007, philanthropy has been an indispensable part of our value system, "Making Life Better."

One Bass Cat and Yar-Craft employee described her more recent volunteer experience as life-changing. "On trips like these, you see people who are so poor they don't even know if they'll have food for that day, but they have such a joy and love of life. Meeting these people first hand has been so overwhelming that it has helped me see others and myself in a new and different way."

Bass Cat and Yar-Craft president Rick Pierce says that the company's service culture shows we are truly caring about others and not just giving lip service. He also believes that the value of these trips isn't limited to just the people we help. "The service trips and the ability to travel have opened the eyes of our participating staff and also presented those aspects to others who have not traveled."

Correct Craft's service trips are designed to benefit not only participants, but also our own circle of friends, family, and co-workers. Lindley Blake, who has planned and organized many of the company's global volunteer initiatives, sees both sides of the coin.

"We truly want to make life better for those who are less fortunate than us. Traveling to where there is need gives us a chance to show love directly by rebuilding a home or improving a school," Lindley observed. "Our volunteer teams have a big heart for service. These trips are intended to help people on a personal level, and also designed to help those within our own circle."

■ ■ ■

An important part of our company culture is the desire to give back to our communities through volunteer service. At Correct Craft headquarters in Orlando, and at each of our companies throughout the United States, hundreds of employees enthusiastically organize each year and carry out volunteer projects that benefit local groups. I'm proud that our teams are so committed to making life better through their community service. They don't just talk about it; they live it out.

At the corporate level, our service programs are focused on a few major Central Florida initiatives, including Habitat for Humanity. Since 2011, we've been partnering with Orlando-based Nautique and Aktion Parks employees to both fund and help build homes for area families. In February 2019, Habitat for Humanity Greater Orlando and Osceola County recognized these teams with its highest honor, the Walter Pharr Legacy Award.

The organization's president and CEO, Catherine Steck McManus, praised our Orlando group for their longtime support. "They have volunteered with us, donated to our mission, advocated on our behalf, and served on our board of directors and committees," she stated. "They are truly a family-focused organization that has reached out to embrace Habitat homeowners and strengthen our community."

In October 2019 we joined up with the *Orlando Sentinel* and launched "Promote Your Passion," a contest that allowed nine local non-profit organizations to each promote their cause through the newspaper's website, expense free. Readers and visitors were able to learn about these groups and vote for the one they believed should win a donation from Correct Craft.

The initiative was a tremendous success. We contributed $5,000 to the top vote getter, Healing Touch Therapeutic Riding Center; $3,000 to our second-place winner, Chance 2 Dance; and a $1,000 contribution to each of the other seven non-profit organizations.

But even more important than our financial contribution was the tremendous visibility we were able to provide these organizations in our Central Florida community. I can think of no finer way to help make life better than by providing visibility and resources for worthy organizations in our community, and I look forward to doing it again.

■ ■ ■

Not surprisingly, our Correct Craft companies each have their own unique approach for making a difference in their own backyards, whether this involves investing time as volunteers, raising money for worthy causes, providing in-kind services, or making charitable donations. It's motivating to see the variety of ways we strive to make life better.

For several years, Orlando-based Nautique and Aktion Parks have focused on causes that are close to their hearts, such as Habitat for Humanity. The Aktion Parks team also takes pride in donating their time and resources to local charities. This has included involvement in such events as First United Methodist's Learning Center Preschool, Play for Purple, St. Jude Foundation, holiday toy drives, and much more. Orlando

Watersports Complex, one of our three watersports parks, recently hosted Above the Wake, an event that teaches the joys of watersports to children with autism.

As new companies have come into the Correct Craft family, it's been inspiring to see them continue and even expand their support for local community projects that appeal to their employees and leadership. For example, last year Pleasurecraft Engine Group employees provided boats powered by PCM and volunteered at two annual events that help create fun days on the lake for kids. Camp Kemo Lake Day allows cancer patients from ages five to eighteen to enjoy boating, tubing, and swimming with their siblings. They also participated in Limitless Sports' annual ski event—a day of adaptive waterskiing, tubing, kayaking, and swimming for participants with special needs.

Pleasurecraft president Mark McKinney said that his team loves serving at these events each year. "Creating a space for children and families to connect and let go of life's hurdles is something we will always want to be part of." Pleasurecraft is also in its sixth year of sponsoring the annual Carolina Sunshine Wishing Well Gala, which raises money to grant wishes for children with uncertain futures.

At Centurion and Supreme, volunteer activities range widely—from supporting Toys for Tots and painting homes for Habitat for Humanity, to visiting retirement homes for an afternoon of arts and crafts. In 2018, more than twenty employees and their families volunteered during the company's Third Annual Lake Clean Up, held at Lake Yosemite in Merced, Calif. They gathered over forty bags of trash at the lake where Centurion and Supreme test their boats and host dealer and customer demo rides.

In 2019 a team of volunteers from Supreme Boats spent the day at Camp Sunshine Dreams, where a fleet of Supremes ferried campers across the lake during the annual camp-wide water fights. The kids enjoyed a carefree afternoon zipping back and forth across the water, battling for lake supremacy. This was the third year in a row the Supreme team was able to participate in Sail Day and help provide a typical sum-mer camp experience for children with cancer. "I'm so proud that our team members are willing to take time out of their day to give back," company president Paul Singer said. "Their dedication and commitment really show how much they care about their community."

In 2020 Bass Cat & Yar-Craft Boats received the Torch Award for Ethics by the Arkansas Better Business Bureau. This award is designed to honor Arkansas companies that demonstrate high standards of business practices aimed to create trust among employees, customers, and their communities. Rewards and recognition for their employees are an important piece in the Bass Cat & Yar-Craft culture that integrates performance, high-character, and ethical behavior.

SeaArk Boats holds a local day of service once or twice a year, usually spending time at one of the area's orphanages. In 2018, SeaArk hosted a back-to-school party for the kids of Arkansas Baptist Children's Home of Monticello, donating food and school supplies and refurbishing some of the center's worn canoes. The following year, they hosted a back-to-school party at Vera Lloyd Presbyterian Family Services, providing lunch along with a Slip 'N Slide and yard games for the children.

"Some of the things these kids have been through is horrible, and to see them laugh or smile will make your month," SeaArk president Steve Henderson observed. "After just a few minutes of interacting with them, you can see they crave that attention and enjoy the time we're there. Although I'm not sure who gets more out of the visit—us or them."

■ ■ ■

Sometimes, we find ourselves making a difference in our communities during times of great adversity. In late March 2020, Correct Craft companies around the country demonstrated true leadership when they stepped up to join in the fight against COVID-19.

For Nautique, it began when we heard from a vendor that COVID-19 had unfortunately forced them to close their business for good. This was a critical supplier who provided material "just in time," so the closure was going to have an immediate impact on our ability to build product. Within twenty-four hours some of our team had repurposed a bay, acquired the right equipment, built workstations, procured the raw materials, and started producing the foam kits in-house.

Correct Craft companies demonstrated this "can do" attitude again and again as they worked to help fill the gap of PPE (personal protective equipment) shortages in their areas. Some examples of this community spirit included Centurion & Supreme Boats' donation of much-needed PPE to supply Memorial Hospital and Doctor's Hospital in Modesto, California. They also made and donated close to a thousand face shields to their local healthcare community. Parker Boats donated N95-certified face masks and protective suits to healthcare facilities in Beaufort, North Carolina.

The Nautique team made an impact by sewing face masks for local healthcare companies. Their upholstery department team offered up home sewing machines to be used as part of the process, while Nautique purchased additional sewing machines and specialty fabric to produce the masks. Orlando Health reached out to Nautique because they had special medical fabric, but no capacity to convert it into masks, so Nautique manufactured those for the hospital as well.

Watershed Innovation and Nautique also partnered to produce medical-quality face shields. Rising to the challenge, employees shifted their efforts from assembling electric motors to cutting down 1,700-pound rolls of plastic donated by Coca-Cola Florida into 80-pound rolls, making it easier for healthcare workers to 3D-print face shields at home.

Our teams are unlike any other. Their drive, creativity, and teamwork to bring so much help and encouragement to their local healthcare communities was inspiring. I'm honored to serve with these people who, even during this devastating crisis, continued working hard at making life better through their community service.

■ ■ ■

The most unique part of Correct Craft's culture is our focus on global outreach. It drives who we are. In fact, it has become so much a part of our culture that a few years ago *Southern Boating* magazine featured one of our service trips and titled the article "Doing the Correct Craft Thing."

As reflected in our mission ("Making Life Better"), I've taken employees on service trips, donating time and resources nearly every year since 2007 to help those in need. Most of these trips are international, but sometimes we work with communities here in the United States as well. It's amazing to see our dedicated employees work so hard for people who will never be able to repay them in any way. It is a true and unselfish service. And the groups we serve love our visits, because we bring engineers, designers, and very talented folks who can make a big difference.

Our first service trip in July 2007 was to Tecate, Mexico, where a team of twenty-one Nautique employees helped build a home for a family of seven. The project was coordinated by Amor Ministries, a non-profit organization in San Diego, California. They had an on-site contractor with plans and pre-cut materials, and put us to work. A year later, in July 2008, Nautique employees traveled back to Tecate, Mexico, and built a new home for a family of four. That same month a group from Nautique went to Nicaragua and volunteered at a homeless shelter for mothers and their children. The team helped with projects around the shelter, and provided the families entertainment and encouragement.

In the aftermath of the devastating Haiti earthquake of January 2010, our employees were already donating items for the Haitian people, but also wanted to volunteer their time. So Nautique teamed up with Missionary Flights International in Fort Pierce, Florida, and spent a day unloading trucks, sorting donations, cleaning bathrooms, and more. Later that year, in July, a group from Nautique traveled to Guatemala City to help the "track people"—families who had settled on abandoned railroad tracks and lived in significant poverty. This team served the group and built them bunk beds.

In July 2011 we took twenty-six employees to the Apache Reservation in Arizona, where we worked on two homes for Apache families in need. We installed windows, beams, and doors, worked on the roofs, and assisted with site clean-up. Our team made a big impact, not only on the homes where we served, but also through helping the organization that builds the houses to develop processes that will benefit them for years, including a new mold they could use on future houses.

The following month, in August 2011, a few employees had the opportunity to visit an organization Nautique has supported in Ethiopia called Project Mercy. This is an incredible organization that's had a dramatic impact on so many lives in that country. A year later, in July 2012, we returned to the Apache Reservation and worked on two separate homes, putting in a ceiling, finishing eaves, and installing a floor. It was tough work, but also fulfilling to assist others in such a significant way.

A small group of Nautique employees visited an African mission in October 2012 and had the opportunity to tour orphanages, schools, a clinic, radio station, vocational school, feeding center, and other services provided by various organizations to the Kenyans and Ugandans.

In July 2013 two Nautique groups traveled to the Dominican Republic, each assigned to a project. The first team spent the early part of the week in downtown Cienfuegos building tables, benches, and chalkboards, and applying a fresh coat of paint to a schoolhouse. The second group worked on a church and a family home in Mocha, about forty-five minutes outside of Santiago. This team helped finish out siding and windows, installed a handrail, and built a stage in the church. Thanks to this great team of volunteers, the family in Mocha had a completed roof for the first time, as well as a door to their home.

In October 2013 we traveled to India to visit the As Our Own project, a community-driven movement that rescues vulnerable children from enslavement and exploitation, and provides lifelong care in a family environment. I had met their president three years earlier in Austria and was inspired to bring a small group to see how we might help. What we saw broke our hearts. Young girls were being taken from their families and trapped in brothels. I had visited many of the poorest places in the world, but this was the worst thing I'd ever seen. It combined unbearable poverty with being assaulted a dozen times a day. Our team decided we had to do more than just visit.

After returning home we came up with a plan to raise money and awareness. The company donated a one-of-a-kind, $120,000 Super Air Nautique G21 boat, which As Your Own raffled off to raise donations. The proceeds helped them continue their good work, giving the rescued girls a chance to get an education and enjoy a brighter future.

In July 2014 two groups of Nautique employees traveled to Ahuachapán, El Salvador to serve those in need. Between them, the teams did construction work for local schools, served in a hospital, and provided food to roughly 600 impoverished families. They also spent time speaking in classrooms and playing sports with the children.

A particularly heart-wrenching experience during this trip was the aid that Nautique's volunteers gave a young woman who'd lost her unborn baby. She didn't have the money to pay for the operation needed to save her own life. Undaunted, the team pitched in and paid for her surgery. Two days later they had an extremely emotional meeting with the young woman.

Three months later, in October 2014, a group of twenty Nautique athletes, dealers, and employees took part in the first-ever Team Nautique service trip to Ahuachapán. This group served by building a boat-shaped school library, which our chief designer helped create using the 3D software on his laptop. They also spent time with the students at the school, passing out supplies and playing soccer with the children. In addition, the team distributed food to more than 400 needy families in rural mountain towns, and provided a water filtration system built to supply the communities with up to one million gallons of fresh water.

This visit led to some remarkable work done on behalf of the community center there. After returning to Orlando, our designer mentioned the project to his supplier in Miami, owner of Rhino Software, who happened to be from El Salvador. He wound up donating to the school $30,000 worth of computers and 3D software licenses, and even went there to teach them how to use it. The end result was the creation of an accredited Design High School program that allows students to learn valuable skills to transform their lives and families.

Another group of employees returned to Ahuachapán again in July 2015. On this trip they built desks for the new CAD Design Center sponsored by Nautique, painted classroom desks and benches, interacted with students, distributed food and clothing to hundreds of families, and visited new mothers in a local maternity ward.

Our dedicated volunteers returned to Haiti in March 2015 to distribute 3,400 pounds of food to hungry Haitians. The Nautique team flew into the Haitian countryside with a plane full of the food, and worked with various organizations to hand it out to local families. They also had an opportunity to review work done by some charitable organizations within Haiti.

That October, several Team Nautique athletes, along with Nautique and Aktion Parks staff, traveled to Cambodia to celebrate the opening of Kam-Air Wake Park—Cambodia's first and only wakeboarding park—with a mission to create liberty for the oppressed through action sports. The team also delivered food to 150 local families working in brick factories, and visited organizations that are fighting human trafficking.

Our second service trip to the Dominican Republic took place in June 2017. With the support of some key vendors—RamLin, CompOne, and DiamondBack—the team was able to help construct a completely custom playground at a local mission camp, Hope 4 DR Now, with headquarters in Puerto Plata, known as Hope Mountain. The playground was fabricated by Nautique and our vendors in the U.S., and then shipped down and assembled on site.

In July 2017 we took thirty employees from Correct Craft, Nautique, SeaArk, Bass Cat, and Centurion Supreme to serve Hosean International Ministries at their Camp De La Grace facility in Pignon, Haiti. While there we built benches for their fellowship building, painted the exteriors of the dormitories, erected two soccer goals, and made electrical system repairs. That Sunday we attended a local church service, and afterward donated food to more than a hundred families.

Steve Henderson, SeaArk's president, came away from this experience feeling that being able to help, even in a small way, can be very big for the soul.

"The Haiti trip was by far the best. The living conditions were bad, but their attitudes were great. One really cool thing I noticed is the bonds that are created between our people on these companywide service trips. Everyone gets a sense of belonging to something bigger than themselves. A lot of lifetime friendships are created there."

In June 2018 we took sixty-three employees to Jamaica to work in a special needs school, NAZ Children's Centre. Employees from Correct Craft, Nautique, SeaArk, Bass Cat, Centurion Supreme, and PCM Engines visited Montego Bay to serve at the private elementary school. We built a pergola with shade sails and picnic tables to serve as an outside eating and gathering area in the school courtyard. The team also built the school a security fence and gate. On Sunday we attended a 180-year-old Jamaican church where we donated some video and sound equipment and food for 150 families, and learned about the community's history and culture.

This was Centurion and Supreme president Paul Singer's first Correct Craft service trip. "It was an honor to see the Correct Craft culture of 'Making Life Better' in Jamaica. I was thrilled that several of our employees participated." The Centurion and Supreme teams are very committed to their local community, he said, but it was also exciting to serve the school in Montego Bay.

A few months later, a group of employees and athletes from Nautique visited the island of Puerto Rico to help rebuild a home that was completely destroyed the previous year by Hurricane Maria. After the trip, Nautique athlete Erika Lang shared her experience:

"To see how much we were able to do in only a few days was unbelievable. The family we helped was so appreciative of everything we did, and it really changed my perspective on things I take for granted in my own life. I'm looking forward to the next service trip."

In January 2019, twenty-eight Correct Craft employees brought hurricane relief to a small community in Florida's panhandle, helping clean up debris and repairing homes impacted by Hurricane Michael. The team also donated tents, cleaning supplies, yard tools, clothing, and medical supplies to area residents. Michael, which had struck the town of Mexico Beach the previous October, was the first Category 4 hurricane to hit Florida's panhandle, and the third-most intense Atlantic hurricane to make landfall in the contiguous United States. Despite its severity, national relief efforts had fallen far short, compared with other major hurricanes'.

Later that year in October, Nautique employees and Orlando-based athletes returned to Puerto Rico to rebuild the home of an elderly couple after it was destroyed in recent hurricanes. Working with a local mission group and the city government, the team built walls, the roof, and front and rear porches with accessible ramps. They installed windows and doors, and ran the electrical wiring. The group used its own money to purchase a new stove, television, linens, and a couch.

In summer 2019 more than 100 Correct Craft employees from across the country traveled to Merced, California—home of our Centurion and Supreme plant—to perform service projects. We called it "Loving on Merced!" and helped by refurbishing the Winton LifeLine Community Center, making repairs at the Applegate Park and Zoo, and providing home repairs for elderly community residents.

"We had thirty-five of our Centurion and Supreme employees use their vacation time to participate in the service trip," noted Centurion and Supreme president Paul Singer. "Working side by side with other Correct Craft employees, they saw lives changed and they shared those observations together at the end of each workday. They have a bond that will last forever, and a heart for service that will change even more lives."

Clearly, service is a critical part of our culture. We want to serve others, and it requires an investment, but the impact on our culture is immeasurable. Our employees know we care and the people who go on these trips are forever impacted. Even those who don't go are inspired, as they hear the stories and realize they work for a company that gives back.

■ ■ ■

I wholeheartedly believe that a company must have a higher mission that drives its values beyond its own success or failure. Your organization has got to have something bigger than coming in every day and punching a time clock. For us, it's helping to make life better for those we can help, both at home and around the globe.

I frequently have people, both inside and outside of the company, tell me our culture is like none they've ever seen or experienced. And while there are many things that influence a culture, I doubt there's anything that impacts it more than service to others.

Our commitment to philanthropy drives who we are and is important to everyone at Correct Craft. I can't begin to express how proud I am of all our companies and employees for the ways they invest their time, money, and ingenuity back into their communities and countries around the world. It thrills me to see them support the Correct Craft culture of service. Our team truly wants to make life better for others.

■ ■ ■

Final Thoughts

Our Correct Craft teams have been given a wonderful platform to make an impact. Over the years, hundreds of our employees have invested time, helping us carry out our philanthropic mission; and while we have been blessed to help others, our team has been just as blessed being able to help.

12

PROMOTING OUR INDUSTRY

Throughout the company's nearly 100-year history, Correct Craft has been dedicated to "Making Life Better" through the three P's—People, Performance, and Philanthropy. Our purpose has never changed. It's the same today as it was in 1925—getting people out on the water to enjoy time with family and friends. We're honored to have served millions of boaters across the globe, helping create nearly a century's worth of treasured memories.

I can't express the importance of being able to spend time on the water with my own family through the years. But it's not just being together that has made our lives better. It's also *where* we've spent that time. Being on and near the water makes a difference.

Scientific research shows that the benefits of boating go far beyond the time spent with our friends and family. In his excellent book, *Blue Mind*, my friend and author Wallace J. Nichols uses many studies and some anecdotal evidence to demonstrate the substantial benefit people receive from being on, near, in, or under the water.

A marine biologist, Dr. Nichols shares lessons in neuroscience—including both standard and advanced medical research using EEGs, MRIs, and fMRIs—to demonstrate water's powerful positive impact. He also uses stories to demonstrate how water not only benefits our overall well-being, but also improves performance in every area of life. The evidence is overwhelming that water positively impacts us in significant ways. The bottom line: people are notably healthier physically, mentally, and emotionally when they are around water. We are also more noticeably calm, creative, inspired, and content there. "Blue Mind" is a powerful concept to which boating gives us access.

■ ■ ■

Not only does boating make life better on a personal level, but our industry is also an important contributor to this country's economy. According to the Bureau of Economic Analysis (BEA), in 2019 the outdoor sector—which includes the recreational boating industry—accounted for 2.2 percent of U.S. GDP, supported 5.2 million American jobs, and contributed $778 billion in gross output.

Compared to other industries the BEA measures, outdoor recreation's economic impact is on par with widely acknowledged stalwarts such as broadcasting and telecommunications, while surpassing other industries commonly recognized as powerhouses. Boating is bigger than mining, utilities, farming and ranching, and chemical products manufacturing.

Equally, if not more important, in 2019 the outdoor recreation economy was growing at 3.9 percent, significantly outpacing the two to four percent growth rate of the overall U.S economy. Boating and fishing alone—the top contributors to the outdoor recreation sector—were enjoyed by more than 141 million Americans that year.

Based on a report conducted by the National Marine Manufacturers Association in 2018, we also know that the boating industry contributed $170.3 billion to the U.S. economy. It supported roughly 35,000 marine businesses—including suppliers, dealers, retailers, repair shops, and marinas—not to mention 691,000 direct and indirect American jobs.

■ ■ ■

I firmly believe that both the personal and economic benefits of spending time on the water are worth preserving and sharing. As head of a major manufacturing company, I feel that it's our responsibility to advocate for the industry and the country's manufacturing sector as well. Over the years, I have used my platform to advocate for boating via newspaper op-eds, industry publication columns and articles, magazine profiles, radio shows, and podcasts.

I've also spent countless hours working with politicians on both the state and national level to help promote and protect the boating public's interests. My involvement in Washington happened a bit by accident. It started with a business trip to Korea, where I met with government officials. After the trip I received a call from the Korean Embassy, indicating that their ambassador to the U.S. would like to visit me in Orlando. He did, and we developed a great rapport, which resulted in me being invited to join him in an Oval Office meeting with President Obama before the signing of the U.S./Korea Free Trade Agreement.

After that meeting with the president, I often got invited to D.C. events, including four more visits to the Obama White House and two visits to the Trump White House. Our team was also honored in late 2017 to host Vice President Pence at our Orlando facility.

During this period, new opportunities to serve came along. As a result of the NMMA promoting me as a candidate, I was appointed to the U.S. Manufacturing Council in 2013 and again in 2015 for two consecutive terms. Along with other business leaders, I advised the Obama administration's Secretary of Commerce, Penny Pritzker, on key issues that directly impact the marine industry. These included innovation, energy, trade, and workforce issues. I also co-chaired the Trade and Tax Policy Committee, which focuses on tax issues that disadvantage U.S. companies and trade opportunities throughout the global marketplace.

Then, in 2019, I was elected chair of the U.S. Interior Department's "Made in America" Outdoor Recreation Advisory Committee. This group, made up of representatives from the outdoor recreation industry, provided counsel to Interior Secretary David Bernhardt on expanding access to and improving infrastructure on public lands and waterways.

I've spent most of my life on, around, and in the water, and almost my entire career in the boating industry. I believe the best way to protect our boating lifestyle is to protect the environment. Even more importantly, I want my kids, future grandkids, and coming generations to enjoy the same water-based lifestyle I have.

It is my sincere desire that the countless trips I've made to Washington, D.C., and Tallahassee, Florida, to advocate for top industry priorities, have made a difference for boat owners across the country. Boating does make life better, and Correct Craft will continue to advocate on behalf of our industry and the boating public when and where it matters most.

■ ■ ■

Final Thoughts

Our Correct Craft platform allows us to serve our industry in a manner that can impact lives positively well beyond our own Correct Craft family. Whether it's at the White House, Capitol Hill, a governor's office, or with community leaders, we appreciate that people listen to us. It is a huge privilege that we take seriously and want to use for the good of our nation, our families, our current and future customers, and our industry.

CONCLUSION

Correct Craft is a unique company with an incredible legacy.

The Meloon family did what few can when they built Correct Craft into a globally respected brand. They navigated through some extremely tough times with the depression, WWII, bankruptcy, and many other challenges. Despite the trials, the family relied on its faith to persevere when many others would have given up.

While the company is much bigger now, the values the Meloon family established still guide us today.

When Daryle Doden became the owner of Correct Craft in 2008 he encouraged us to not only embrace the company's historical values, but to double down on them. I appreciate the trust he has displayed in me and our team as we grow Correct Craft and work to provide not only financial returns, but also cultural and eternal returns.

During the past fourteen years that I have been honored to lead Correct Craft, there has never been a "normal" year. We navigated through the company's sale right into the Great Recession. For nearly a decade, we have experienced explosive growth through both organic expansion and acquisitions that resulted in a long string of record years. As I write this, we are managing through COVID-19. Fortunately, we have a great team that keeps stepping up to excel at anything they undertake.

Speaking of our team, I don't have the words to describe the appreciation I feel for them. Those who know me best understand that I am likely the least talented person on our team, and I deeply appreciate those whom I work with at Correct Craft and our companies. They are exceptional.

I have heard it said that CEO's get too much blame when things go bad and too much credit when things go well. I can say for sure that whatever accolades have come my way are a result of a lot of people working together. I love our team!

Thanks for reading our story.

ABOUT THE AUTHOR

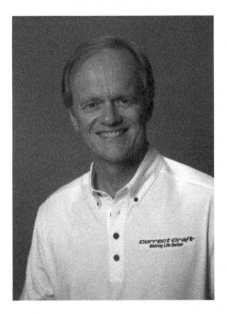

Bill Yeargin is the CEO of Correct Craft. Under Bill's leadership, Correct Craft has won all their industry's major awards and developed a unique culture of "Making Life Better." A passionate lifelong learner, Bill earned an MBA and completed post-graduate education at Harvard, Stanford, Villanova, and MIT.

Having served both the Obama and Trump administrations on cabinet-level advisory councils, *Florida Trend* magazine recognized Bill as one of "Florida's Most Influential Business Leaders."

Bill has been published hundreds of times, has authored four books, and is a sought-after conference speaker.

He and his wife Leigh have two daughters, Erin (married to Ben) and Amanda.